Illustrating GREAT WORDS

OF THE NEW TESTAMENT

J. B. FOWLER, JR.

BROADMAN PRESS
NASHVILLE, TENNESSEE

© Copyright 1991 ● Broadman Press
All rights reserved
4250-93
ISBN: 0-8054-5093-9
Dewey Decimal Classification: 225
Subject Heading: BIBLE, NEW TESTAMENT
Library of Congress Card Catalog Number: 90-33348
Printed in the United States of America

Library of Congress Cataloging-in-Publication Data
Fowler, J. B., 1930-
  Illustrating great words of the New Testament / J.B. Fowler.
  p. cm.
  ISBN: 0-8054-5093-9 :
  1. Homiletical illustrations. 2. Bible. N.T.--Homiletical use.
  I. Title.
  BV4225.2.F67 1990
  252'.08--dc20

                                                    90-33348
                                                    CIP

Faith: 55-56

" : 56-57

Fear: 58

Forgiveness: 60-61

Jesus: 68

To my friends and co-workers in the Baptist Convention of New Mexico, and especially to Executive Director Claude Cone and my co-workers in the Baptist Building in Albuquerque. A special appreciation is expressed to my secretary, Lisa Francis, who painstakingly typed the manuscript.

Heaven: 70-71

" : 73-74

Joy/Happiness 99

Keeping: Secure: 106 107

Contents

Preface 9
Foreword 11
Adoption. 13
Angels. 15
Anger 17
Assurance/Security 19
Baptize/Baptism. 23
Believe. 26
Blood. 29
Born Again. 32
Burdens. 36
Careful/Anxious. 39
Church 41
Cross. 45
Death 49
Example 52
Faith 55
Fear. 58
Forgiveness. 60
Foundation 63
God. 64
Grace. 67
Heaven 70
Hell 75
Home 78
Honesty. 81
Hope 84
Humble/Humility 87
Idle/Idleness. 90
Immortality 91
Jealous/Jealousy. 93
Jesus/Christ 95
Joy. 99

Judgment 102
Kind/Kindness....................................... 105
Laugh/Laughter...................................... 109
Lost.. 111
Love 114
Man/Woman 119
Mercy 123
Miracles 126
Neglect 129
Peace... 131
Prayer 134
Pride 137
Redeem/Redemption................................... 139
Repent/Repentance 143
Resurrection/Easter................................. 146
Sacrifice... 150
Salvation 153
Satan/Devil 158
Scriptures/Bible 161
Sin... 166
Sowing/Reaping...................................... 171
Suffering/Trials 175
Temptation 178
Trust 181
Unbelief.. 184
Witness/Witnessing 186
Index... 189

Preface

A church secretary in New Jersey was preparing the Sunday bulletin and when she asked her pastor for his sermon title, he said: "Next Sunday morning I am going to preach on the theme, 'Are Ministers Cracking Up?'"

The secretary looked a bit puzzled when she heard the title, but she was hesitant to ask too many questions about the pastor's sermon. After all, she thought, that was between the pastor and God.

So she printed the bulletins and when they were distributed the following Sunday morning, at the appropriate place in the order of service the sermon was announced: "*Our* Minister's Cracking Up."

Preparing three or four sermons each week as most evangelical pastors do is enough to make a fellow "crack up." Add to this all the pastor's administrative duties, his civic responsibilities, his counseling ministry—to say nothing about hospital visitation, funerals, and marriages—and the first thing the pastor knows, it has turned into a full-time job!

Preparing sermons is in itself a full-time job. If a preacher didn't have anything to do but prepare two sermons for Sunday, he would really have more than he could do. More than he could do, that is, if he were conscientious about sermon preparation.

When I was a boy I once heard my pastor say a thing I didn't understand. One Sunday morning he announced he was going to preach a sermon on which he had been working for sixteen years!

Today, after having preached for forty years, I understand what he was saying. The sermon goes through a birth process: conception, gestation, and delivery. Much of this process is the mental "chewing" of a text, the mulling of it in one's mind until it is understood so well that the sermon can be put down on paper and then delivered in a worship service.

That's where I hope this book will be useful. None of these illustrations is new or original. I have collected them over the years from scores of sources. But they are good, solid illustrations that the preacher can use to season his sermon as did the One who "spoke nothing except by parables."

The late Dr. J. D. Grey of the First Baptist Church of New Orleans in his book *Epitaphs for Eager Preachers*, tells about a preacher whose church custodian found an order of service left in the sanctuary from the previous Sunday. On it were written these words:

> I never see my pastor's eyes
> Though they with light may shine;
> For when he prays he closes his,
> And when he preaches, mine.[1]

The pastor, apparently, had not learned the value of a good story. Do you know anything, other than a short sermon, that will come nearer keeping your people awake and holding their attention on Sunday than a good illustration? In this book you will find one or two that fall into that category.

Take these illustrations and use them. For all those both named and unnamed from whom I have borrowed them, I express my sincerest thanks.

1. J. D. Grey, *Epitaphs for Eager Preachers* (Nashville: Broadman Press, 1972), 122.

Foreword

The New Testament is a book of enriched and enriching words that was written in the Greek language, a language never excelled to express many shades and nuances of meaning in a single word. Often it takes more than an English sentence to express the luminous truth in a single word from the Greek New Testament.

Dr. Fowler's illustrations open windows and allow light to pour in on the words of the New Testament. Some of his illustrations are like street lamps showing the way. Others are like Tiffany lamps, presenting many colors in a single word. Still others of his stories are like spotlights which single out and bathe in brightness words from the New Testament.

A major purpose of illustrating is to make the truth memorable. A single, well-selected anecdote or story can rivet the truth to the human mind more than paragraphs of technical explanation. Dr. J. B. Fowler, a master editor and himself a wordsmith as well as a painter with words, provided us a valuable tool and resource in illustrating great words of the New Testament. A picture is indeed worth a thousand words and he has given us some beautiful word pictures.

Joel Gregory, Pastor
Travis Avenue Baptist Church,
Fort Worth, Texas

Adoption

But ye have received the Spirit of adoption, whereby we cry, Abba, Father (Rom. 8:15).

In his *Studies in the Vocabulary of the Greek New Testament*, Kenneth Wuest says that the word "adoption" is a combination of two words that are translated "son" and "to place." Thus, according to Wuest, adoption means, "to place as a son."

Wuest continues:

It (adoption) was a term used in Roman legal practice. It referred to a legal action by which a person takes into his family a child not his own, with the purpose of treating him as and giving him all the privileges of an own son. The custom was not common among the Jews, but was so among the Romans, with whom an adopted child is legally entitled to all rights and privileges of a natural-born child. This custom, well-known in the Roman empire, is used in the N. T., as an illustration of the act of God giving a believing sinner, who is not His natural child, a position as His adult son in the family. This is a legal act and position, and not the same as regeneration and a place in the family as a born-child of God.[1]

Donald Grey Barnhouse in his book *Let Me Illustrate*, explains the Pauline concept of adoption by citing an illustration from *The Robe* by Lloyd C. Douglas.

Lucia describes the ceremony held for her older brother in which he was acknowledged publicly as the son of his father.

Lucia's father had bought Demetrius, who was a Corinthian slave, six years earlier and had given the slave to Marcellus for his seventeenth birthday.

As they all assemble in the forum to see Marcellus step forward to receive the white toga of sonship, his father and Cornelius Capito make speeches. Then they place the white toga on Marcellus's shoulders.

Sister Lucia is so proud and happy that she is nearly beside herself with joy. But she is only nine and she knows that Marcellus is much older and must act like a man.

As Marcellus is inducted into manhood, his father makes a speech welcoming him into Roman citizenship and Marcellus's eyes fill with tears. Then Cornelius Capito makes a patriotic speech reminding Marcellus that Mother Rome deserves young Marcellus' finest loyalty and commitment. Thus, with the ceremony and the placing of the white toga on Marcellus' shoulders, he is publicly acknowledged as a son, introduced to manhood and to citizenship in the Roman Empire.

This is something of what the New Testament word "adoption" means. It is not simply the bringing of another child into the family. Rather, it is the welcoming of a grown-up man or a grown-up woman into the family. They are welcomed into the family with all the rights of a grown-up with full citizenship. Thus we come into God's family not quaking in fear of Him, but as grown-up children who have come of age, and are publicly acknowledged as sons and daughters of God.[2]

1. Kenneth Wuest, *Studies in the Vocabulary of the Greek New Testament* (Grand Rapids, Mich.: Wm. B. Eerdmans Publishing Co., 1955) 78-79. Used by permission.

2. Donald Grey Barnhouse, *Let Me Illustrate* (Westwood, N. J.: Fleming H. Revell Co., 1967), 19.

Angels

But to which of the angels said he at any time, Sit on my right hand, until I make thine enemies thy footstool? Are they not all ministering spirits, sent forth to minister for them who shall be heirs of salvation? (Heb. 1:13-14).

I once heard actor Mickey Rooney tell about an experience he had before he became a Christian. He was entertaining at a hotel in Lake Tahoe, Nevada, and when he went down to breakfast one morning a busboy with long golden hair and wearing a white jacket suddenly walked up to Rooney's table. Without introducing himself, the young man said: "Mr. Rooney, I want you to know how much Jesus Christ loves you." With that, the busboy disappeared.

When Rooney went to pay his breakfast check, he inquired of the lady at the cash register about the busboy with the golden hair because, Rooney said, he wanted to talk to the boy. But the cashier said no such person worked there. Mickey Rooney went on to say to millions of people watching by television that he believes it was an angel who appeared to him.

In his book *Angels, God's Secret Agents,* Billy Graham says that the Bible says more about angels than it does about the devil or demons. Drawing from a story originally printed in *Reader's Digest,* Graham tells about an experience Dr. S. W. Mitchell, a celebrated Philadelphia neurologist, had a good many years ago.

Dr. Mitchell had gone to bed "after an exceptionally tiring day. Suddenly he was awakened by someone knocking on his door. Opening it he found a little girl, poorly dressed and deeply upset. She told him her mother was very sick and asked him if he would please come with her. It was a bitterly cold, snowy night, but though he was bone tired, Dr. Mitchell dressed and followed the little girl."

Graham continues:

> He found the mother desperately ill with pneumonia. After arranging for medical care, he complimented the sick woman on the intelligence and persistence of her little daughter. The woman looked at him strangely and then said, "My daughter died a month ago." She added, "Her shoes and coat are in the clothes closet there." Dr. Mitchell, amazed and perplexed, went to the closet and opened the door. There hung the very coat worn by the little girl who had brought him to attend to her mother. It was warm and dry and could not possibly have been out in the wintry night.

"Could the doctor have been called in the hour of desperate need by the angel who appeared as this woman's young daughter? Was this the work of God's angel on behalf of the sick woman?" Graham asks.[1]

Graham also tells a story about revered pioneer missionary John G. Paton who served in the New Hebrides Islands. Paton's missionary home was surrounded one night by hostile natives who were going to burn out the missionaries and kill them. All through the frightening night Paton and his wife prayed for God's deliverance. With the coming of daylight, the Patons watched the would-be attackers leave.

The chief of the tribe became a Christian about a year later. Missionary Paton asked the chief what had kept them from burning down the missionary's house and killing them, and the chief replied: "Who were all those men you had with you there?"

Paton replied that no one was there except himself and his wife, but the chief said he had seen hundreds of big men in shining clothing holding drawn swords standing in a circle around the mission station.

Paton said they were God's angels sent to protect His servants.[2]

1. Billy Graham, *Angels, God's Secret Agents* (Waco, Tex.: Word Publishing, Inc., 1975), 2-3.
2. Ibid., 2-3 (adapted).

Anger

Let all bitterness, and wrath and anger, . . . be put away from you (Eph. 4:31).

Once Abraham Lincoln's secretary of state, William Henry Seward, wrote a scathing letter to an army contractor who was stealing from the government. When Seward showed it to Lincoln, the President said: "It's not half strong enough." So Seward wrote a second letter to the contractor in which he ate him alive.

"That serves the thief right," Lincoln said upon seeing the letter.

"Very well," Seward said, "I will mail it immediately."

"Oh, no," the patient Lincoln replied. "Don't mail it. Throw it in the wastebasket."[1]

Booker T. Washington (1856-1915) was a great Afro-American educator. He organized the famous Tuskegee Institute, a school for Afro-Americans, at Tuskegee, Alabama. He was the school's first president.

Washington was born in slavery at Hales Fort, Virginia. Although he attended a mission school, he was largely self-educated. Few people have influenced the black race as much as did Washington.

On one occasion Washington was invited to give an address in a large city. Hailing a cab, Washington asked the driver to take him to the auditorium where Washington was to speak. But the white driver refused because Washington was black.

Patiently addressing the prejudiced driver, Washington said: "Alright, then, if you will get in the passenger seat I will drive you to the auditorium."[2]

Another great Afro-American educator who refused to be victimized by anger was George Washington Carver (1864-1943). Like Booker T. Washington, Carver was also born a slave. A renowned scientist who taught at Tuskegee Institute from 1896 until his death, Dr. Carver developed more than 300 products from the peanut alone. From the pecan, he produced 75 salable products. And from the sweet potato he developed 118 products. It is likely he saved Southern agriculture from destruction by diversifying from cotton.

On one occasion Carver was interviewed by a newspaper reporter. When the interview appeared in the paper, it was not very complimentary toward Carver. Among other things the reporter could have left out of the story was the statement that Dr. Carver was "a toothless old man."

But when Carver read the interview, his reply was: "I am not toothless; I had my teeth right here in my pocket all through the interview."[3]

In his book *Ideas and Illustrations for Inspirational Talks*, Jack Gulledge quotes Dr. Redford B. Williams Jr., a Duke University scientist, who said that studies "suggest that an awful lot of premature mortality may be associated with hostility."

Williams wrote that hostility and anger may be a dangerous key component of the heart attack-prone type-A individual—ambitious, impatient men and women.

"Half of the American population is considered type A, and the incident of heart disease in this type is five times higher among hostile people than those who are more relaxed."[4]

1. Bill Thorn, *Wake Up, Make Up and Go* (Newton, Kans.: United Printing, 1971), 99.
2. Jack Finegan, *At Wit's End* (Richmond, Va.: John Knox Press, 1963), 74.
3. Ibid.
4. Jack Gulledge, *Ideas and Illustrations for Inspirational Talks* (Nashville: Broadman Press, 1986), 6.

Assurance / Security

Let us draw near with a true heart in full assurance of faith (Heb. 10:22).

English writer Guy King tells about seeing a little girl standing on the curb of a very busy street. She wanted to cross the street, but she was inexperienced, the traffic was heavy, and she was afraid. King said before he could get to the little girl to help her across the street, a big, strong policeman came up and reached out for the hand of the little girl. Putting her little hand in his big hand, the two of them stepped out into the street.

King said that he was sure the heart of the little girl was still trembling and that her whole body was shaking as they crossed the busy street, but they moved ahead and soon were safe on the other side. The little girl's safety, King added, did not depend upon her hold on the policeman, but his hold on her.[1]

Arthur Hugh Clough wrote about it this way:

"It fortifies my soul to know
That though I perish, truth is so;
That, wheresoe'er I stray and range,
Whate'er I do, Thou dost not change.
I steadier step when I recall
That, if I slip, Thou dost not fall."[2]

The Golden Gate Bridge connecting Northern California to San Francisco is one of the most spectacular bridges in the world. The two massive towers, 1,125 feet apart, hold the two thirty-six-and-a-half inch cables from which the bridge is suspended. The six-lane bridge was completed in May 1937 at a cost of $35.5 million.

During the first phase of construction, so it is related, there were no safety nets beneath the workers and twenty-three men fell to their deaths in the water below. But during the second phase of construction, a safety net was installed at a cost of $100,000, saving the lives of at least ten men who fell while working. During the second phase of construction, work was done 15 to 25 percent more quickly because the workmen had the assurance that if they fell, they would survive.[3]

Those who are truly trusting in Jesus as their personal Saviour can have full assurance of eternal life. Jesus promised: "And I give unto them eternal life; and they shall never perish, neither shall any man pluck them out of my hand" (John 10:28).

It is related that on the morning after the assassination of President Abraham Lincoln, 50,000 mourners gathered in downtown New York City.

As the emotions of the crowd began to rise and it was feared that violence stemming from anger over Lincoln's death might erupt, a man stepped out on the balcony of an adjacent building and called out loudly: "Fellow citizens! Clouds and darkness are around about Him (God). His pavillion is dark waters, and thick clouds of the skies. Justice and judgment are the establishment of His throne. Mercy and truth go before His face. Fellow citizens! God reigns and the government of Washington still lives!"

The speaker was James A. Garfield who would become president in 1881 and be assassinated on July 2 of that same year.[4]

W. A. Criswell is pastor of the First Baptist Church of Dallas. In his book *These Issues We Must Face*, he tells about a terrible period of doubt through which he passed when he was a young pastor.

Dr. Criswell said that he was saved at a revival meeting as a small child. It was a 10 AM service when he made his profession of faith in the Lord Jesus. Humbly and simply, only as a child could do it, Dr. Criswell said that he gave his heart and life to the Savior.

He began to preach in rural areas when he was only seventeen years old. In conducting revival meetings out in the country churches during the early days of his ministry, Criswell was amazed at the marvelous testimonies that he heard from the lips of those devout, rural people.

One day one of his deacons took him to a place and said to the young pastor: "Do you see that spot right there? After mourning for my sins for many years, and after carrying an intolerable burden on my soul, I was standing in that place when suddenly there came from heaven a great ball of fire and burst over my head. I fell to the ground and how long I lay in that state I do not know, but when I came to myself the burden of my sins had rolled away."[5]

He then described for Dr. Criswell how the whole world looked new to him—how the mules looked when he was plowing; how the birds sang in the trees; how the whole landscape outlook changed; and how things were different at home and in the family.

Criswell said that after having listened to such testimonies he came to the conclusion that he had never been saved and that he did not know the Lord. He was saved as any child is saved—humbly and simply trusting Jesus the best he knew how. But he felt that his experience was totally inadequate.

The early years of his ministry were agony. He was trying to preach the gospel to others, but secretly he feared that he did not know the Lord. Night after night he cried to God in his bedroom and asked for some kind of sign whereby he might know that he had really been saved. During those agonizing days he cried out to God in prayer and read through His holy Word that he might find assurance for his soul. Finally, that assurance was given to him in a judgment scene.

Criswell said that when the judgment day comes, and he stands before the Savior and Jesus asks him by what right he dares to make claim to eternal life and admittance to heaven, if he answers that it is because he saw an angel of light from heaven, that Satan will laugh and answer: "So he saw an angel from heaven! I was that angel of light. I transformed myself into an angel of light just to fool you. Come, you belong to me." (see 2 Cor. 11:14)

But, he said, On that great and final day when I stand before the Lord of all the earth, and he asks me by what right I dare to claim eternal life and admittance to the heavenly city, I shall answer:

I know that I have been born again because I am trusting in the Lord Jesus Christ to save me, and because you say in your word: "But as many as received him, to them gave he the power to become the sons of God, even to them that believe on his name." Now, Lord Jesus, it's up to you to keep your word which I accepted by faith.[6]

Have you ever been there? Have you ever passed through those dark and deep waters of doubt? Well, if you have, then you can appreciate the peace and assurance that finally came to Dr. Criswell when he knew in his heart that he had, indeed, really been born again.

1. Guy King, *Salvation Symphony* (London and Edinburgh: Marshall, Morgan, and Scott, Ltd., 1946), 110.

2. Nenien C. McPherson, Jr., *The Power of Purpose* (Old Tappan, N. J.: Fleming H. Revell Co., 1959), 37.

3. Walter B. Knight, *Knight's Master Book of New Illustrations* (Grand Rapids, Mich.: William B. Eerdmans Publishing Co., 1956), 14.

4. Ibid, 20.

5. W. A. Criswell, *These Issues We Must Face* (Grand Rapids, Mich.: Zondervan, 1953), 110.

6. Ibid, 111.

Baptize / Baptism

And they went down both into the water, both Philip and the eunuch; and he baptized him (Acts 8:38).

Charles Haddon Spurgeon, probably the greatest preacher since Paul, was reared in a Congregational home. Both his father and grandfather were preachers.

Spurgeon was converted in 1850 when he was fifteen, on a cold, snowy Sunday morning in Colchester, England.

Driven that Sunday morning into the Primitive Methodist Church to escape the fierce winter storm, Spurgeon listened to the unlettered, shoemaker preacher as he spoke to no more than a dozen people.

Announcing his text, "Look unto me and be ye saved, all the ends of the earth" (Isa. 45:22), the preacher looked squarely at Spurgeon. "You are in trouble, young man, and you'll never get out of it unless you look to Jesus . . . Look! Look! Look!" he shouted.

That morning, Spurgeon, who was destined to preach to tens of thousands of people from his great Metropolitan Baptist Tabernacle in London, was saved.

On May 3, 1851, Spurgeon was baptized in the River Lark. It was his mother's birthday. The water and weather were so cold that a fire was built by the people standing on the banks so they could keep warm. Spurgeon, then sixteen, had walked eight miles that morning to be baptized.

His mother said she had often prayed that Spurgeon might be converted. "But I never asked that you would be a Baptist," she confessed. Blocked from attending Cambridge because he was an outcast Baptist in Anglican England, Spurgeon set himself to reading, study, and prayer.

Not only did he preach to great throngs in London's 5,000-seat Metropolitan Tabernacle, but for forty years in England, Europe, and America, his sermons sold 150 million copies. In addition, he wrote 135 books translated into many languages.

God used Spurgeon mightily. Only five feet, six inches tall, Spurgeon was bearded, stocky, and had a magnificent voice. And for twenty years his wife was a bed-ridden invalid.[1]

> Ann and Adoniram Judson were the first Baptist foreign missionaries from the United States. He was a Congregationalist minister reared in Massachusetts, who sailed with his wife for India in February 1812. But as he sailed toward India (and a meeting with Baptist missionary William Carey), Judson studied his New Testament and came to the conviction that only those who were responsible should be baptized and that it should be by immersion. So, when he and his wife landed at Calcutta, they were both baptized by immersion and sent word back to the American Congregational Board in Massachusetts that they were now Baptists.[2]

Jack Gulledge in his book *Ideas and Illustrations for Inspirational Talks*, has a helpful illustration about baptism.

"The River Jordan flows southward through the Holy Land. For the most part it is neither beautiful nor peaceful. It's 25 percent mud and plunges downhill at a furious pace, falling nine feet per mile.

"The 158-mile river begins in the snows of Mount Hermon at a point 260 feet above sea level. By the time it empties into the Dead Sea, at a point 1,287 feet below sea level, the water has reached the lowest point on earth.

"Ironically, the river that has inspired thousands of hymns sung by millions the world over, and on whose banks the words were uttered that influenced the course of mankind, today serves as a barrier for thirty miles for the hostile nations of Israel and Syria.

"Amid the unbeautiful, sometimes furious river, east of Jericho, there is a lovely bend called Makhadet-Al-Hijla, or the Ford of the Partridge. It's a place of great beauty, shaded by willows and eucalptus trees, much as it was in New Testament times. Here, according to tradition, Jesus was baptized by John the Baptist.

"How symbolic. The place of our baptism is a spot of beauty and peace amid a furious flowing river of hate and strife. When Jesus was confronted by those who sought to take Him, He 'went away again beyond Jordan into the place where John at first baptized; and there he abode' (John 10:40).

"Whether at this location on the Jordan, or another, Jesus found refuge from the trials of life, at the place of His baptism. And we can, too. When difficulties seem more than we can bear, going back to our baptismal experience puts it all in perspective."[3]

1. Benjamin P. Browne, *Tales of Baptist Daring* (Philadelphia, Chicago, and Los Angeles: Judson Press, 1961), 119-123.

2. See the author's book, *Illustrated Sermons for Special Occasions* (Nashville: Broadman Press, 1988), 111-112.

3. Jack Gulledge, *Ideas and Illustrations for Inspirational Talks* (Nashville: Broadman Press, 1986), 10-11.

Believe

Believe on the Lord Jesus Christ, and thou shalt be saved (Acts 16:31).

Harold T. Bryson recounts the well-known story of Blondin, a famous tightrope walker who lived in the latter part of the 19th century. The story appears in James E. Hightower's book, *Illustrating Paul's Letter to the Romans.*

Once Blondin strung a tightrope across the Niagara Falls. Thousands of curious onlookers had gathered to watch Blondin walk the tightrope from the Canadian to the American side of the falls. Thousands cheered his name as he stepped on the high rope.

Silencing the crowd, Blondin said to them, "I am going to walk across the Niagara Falls on the tightrope, but this time I will carry someone on my shoulders. Do you believe in me?"

"We believe! We believe!" shouted the excited crowd.

"Then which of you will be the lucky person to have Blondin carry him across the falls?" Blondin asked.

Heavy silence fell over the crowd. But in a few minutes one of the onlookers moved slowly toward Blondin, climbed up on his shoulders, and had the thrill of his life as Blondin carried him safely across to the American side of the falls..

All the people agreed that they believed Blondin could do it, but only one man believed in Blondin enough to trust him.[1]

Leslie Weatherhead draws a good distinction between "believe" and "believe in."

Let us note the difference between the expressions "believe" and "believe in," the difference between believing things about a person and believing in a person; the difference between agreeing with what a person says or does and believing in a person's integrity and character. I have one friend who is outstanding because I hardly agree with him about anything—theology, politics or literature—and yet I believe in him intensely. I don't believe what he says, but I believe in him. In a word, I trust him.[2]

Presbyterian missionary John G. Paton sailed to the South Sea Islands in 1858. For a while, he served on the small island of Aniwa where his life was constantly in danger from murderers and cannibals. After a great outpouring of God's grace upon the island, Paton described it as the most open and reverent Christian community that he had ever visited. Paton's life and ministry, one author states, was like "a perpetual miracle."

In the New Hebrides Islands of the Pacific, Paton could not find a word in the native language for the word "believe," meaning trust. Trying to translate the encounter of Paul with the Philippian jailer in Acts 16, Paton came to the verse, "What must I do to be saved?"

The apostle answered the Philippian jailer with the simple words, "Believe on the Lord Jesus Christ and thou shalt be saved."

When Paton got to that verse and tried to translate the word "believe," he finally settled upon this: "Lean your whole weight upon the Lord Jesus Christ and be saved."

Isn't that what it means to believe on Jesus?

Edgar DeWitt Jones says there are more than a thousand references in the Bible to the heart. Jones says that in some places in the Scriptures when "heart" is used, "intellect" is meant. In other places, "heart" indicates, as Jones puts it, "the will faculty." But most of the places in the Bible that "heart" is used, Jones says "the whole man is meant, with the affections as the ruling quality."[3]

Believing with the "heart" is the only way to be saved (Romans 10:9-10).

1. James E. Hightower, *Illustrating Paul's Letter to the Romans* (Nashville: Broadman Press, 1984), 31-32.
2. Leslie Weatherhead, *20 Centuries of Great Preaching Vol. XI* (Dallas, Tex.: Word

Books, Inc., 1971), 125. Used by permission.

3. Edgar DeWitt Jones, *Sermons I Love to Preach* (New York and San Franbcisco: Harper & Row, Publishers, Inc., 1953 and 1981), 160-61. Reprinted by permission of the publisher.

Blood

And the blood of Jesus Christ his Son cleanseth us from all sin (1 John 1:7).

The brother of Escalus, a Roman soldier, was condemned because of his crimes. Standing before Caesar whom he had served well and on whose behalf he had often been wounded, Escalus pled, "On behalf of these scars, pardon my brother."

Martin Luther, the Protestant reformer, once had a dream in which he stood before God on the day of judgment and Satan was there to confront Luther.

Satan, always the accuser, looked at the open books and pointed to Luther's many sins and his heart sank in despair. Remembering the cross, Luther rebuked Satan: "There is one entry which you did't make, Satan," Luther said.

"And what is that one?" the devil sneered.

"It is this one," answered Luther: "The blood of Jesus Christ his Son cleanseth us from all sin" (1 John 1:7).[1]

Frances Ridley Havergal was one of our great Christian hymn writers. We have sung her hymns: "Like A River Glorious"; "I Am Trusting Thee, Lord Jesus"; "Take My Life and Let It Be"; "I Gave My Life For Thee"; and "Who Is On The Lord's Side?"

According to author F. J. Huegel, Havergal had long been burdened with shame because of her many sins. However, one day as she was reading her Greek New Testament she came to 1 John 1:7: "And the blood of Jesus Christ his Son cleanseth us from all sin."

When she discovered that "cleanseth" is in the present tense—continuous, never-ending action—Havergal realized that the blood of Christ forever was cleansing her. Her joy then became full and unspeakable.

When Havergal died, her Bible lay open on the casket to 1 John 1:7. It was her favorite verse.[2]

The late Harold John Ockenga wrote:

> The atonement is represented by the cross of Christ. This is evidenced from the synonymous use of the phrase "the cross of Christ" and the phrase "the death of Christ" and the phrase "the blood of Christ." In fact, the blood of Christ is mentioned three times as often as the death of Christ, and five times as often as the cross of Christ. No doubt this is because the Bible declares "without the shedding of blood there is no remission of sin" (Heb. 9:22). The shedding of blood is connected with an atonement for sin.[3]

William Barclay says that according to W. D. Davies in his book *Paul and Rabbinic Judaism,* that in the temple at Jerusalem every year there were sacrificed 1093 lambs, 113 bulls, 37 rams and 32 goats. These were the "official" sacrifices and do not count the "private" sacrifices.[4]

An old English herdsman was critically ill and was taken to a London hospital. His family knew he could never get well and return home, so they visited him regularly. His little granddaughter was a particular comfort to him.

One day she was reading to him from the epistle of 1 John when she came to verse seven: "And the blood of Jesus Christ his son cleanseth us from all sin."

Upon hearing those words, the old man raised up on one arm and asked his little granddaughter, "Are those words there, Honey? Are you sure they are there?"

"Yes, Grandpa," the little girl answered. "They are right here where I am reading."

"Then, child, read them to me again for I have never heard anything like that," he pled.

After she had read the promise again, the old man asked a second time:

"Honey, are you sure those words are there?"

"Yes, Grandpa," she patiently answered. "Look, they are right here where my finger is."

Then her Grandpa said very reverently: "Then if anyone shall ask you how Grandpa died, you tell them that he died believing in the words you just read to me: 'And the blood of Jesus Christ his son cleanseth us from all sin.' "[5]

They were the old man's last words. Slowly his head fell back on the pillow and he went home to be with Jesus.

1. Clarence E. Macartney, *Macartney's Illustrations* (New York and Nashville: Abington-Cokesbury Press, 1945), 35.

2. F. J. Huegel, *The Cross Through The Scriptures* (Grand Rapids, Mich.: Zondervan Publishing House, 1966), 155.

3. Harold John Ockenga, *Preaching For Today* (Grand Rapids, Mich.: Wm. B. Eerdmans Publishing Co. 1959), pp. 115-116. Used by permission.

4. William Barclay, *A Spiritual Autobiography* (Grand Rapids, Mich.: Wm. B. Eerdmans Publishing Co., 1975), 92.

5. Elon Foster, *6000 Classic Sermon Illustrations* (Grand Rapids, Mich.: Baker Book House, 1974), 86.

Born Again

Marvel not that I said unto thee, Ye must be born again (John 3:7).

Since Abraham Lincoln never joined a church, many have wondered if he was a Christian. In his book *Abraham Lincoln: The Man and His Faith,* G. Frederick Owen relates that Lincoln was, indeed, a Christian.

Lincoln attended revival services in 1850 at the First Presbyterian Church in Springfield, Ill. During the revival Mrs. Lincoln presented herself on profession of faith, Owen relates. She had been a member of the Episcopal Church since she was confirmed at twelve years of age, but she confessed she had never been saved until she made her commitment to Christ in the Presbyterian revival.

Lincoln did not make a public commitment to Jesus during the revival. Reverend James F. Jacquess, the pastor of Springfield's First Methodist Church, related that he knew for certain Lincoln had been born again.

One Sunday morning Lincoln attended the Methodist Church and clung to the words of the preacher as he spoke from John 3: "Ye must be born again." Jacquess said Lincoln paid very close attention to the message and a few days later Lincoln called upon the preacher to talk more about those words of Jesus. Jacquess said he believed Lincoln was saved that night as they talked.

Hy. Pickering, tells in his book *Twice-Born Men*, that Lincoln was once asked by "a friend" if he loved Jesus. President Lincoln buried his face in his handkerchief and "wept and sobbed," Pickering relates. Lincoln then confessed that when he came to the presidency he was not a Christian. Not even after the death of three-year-old Eddie, his and Mary's little son who had died on February 1, 1850, was Lincoln saved.

Continuing, Lincoln said that when he went to Gettysburg on November 19, 1863, to make his now well-known Gettysburg Address, he pondered the graves of those brave men and "then and there" trusted in Christ as his Savior. Lincoln added, "I do love Jesus."[1]

Pickering relates that someone had an appointment with Lincoln at 5 AM and arrived at Lincoln's office fifteen monutes early. While waiting to see the president, the visitor heard someone inside the office talking aloud. When he inquired who was talking, the president's attendant replied that it was Mr. Lincoln. The caller asked if someone was with Lincoln. No, the attendant replied, Lincoln was alone. He made a habit of reading his Bible and praying each morning from 4 AM to 5 AM.[2]

Charles G. Finney (1790-1875) was a lawyer who became a Presbyterian and Congregationalist evangelist.

Finney says he was born again while he was in law school. One day while sitting in an office alone, Finney said the Lord asked, "Finney, what are you going to do when you get your law degree?"

Finney said he answered: "I'll begin to practice law."

The voice of the Lord seemed to ask Finney, "Then what are you going to do?"

And Finney replied that he hoped he would get rich.

"Then what are you going to do?" the voice of the Lord asked.

And Finney replied, "Then I will retire and take it easy."

"What then?" the Lord asked.

And Finney replied, "Then I'll die, Lord."

"Then what, Finney?" the voice of the Lord asked.

Finney replied, "Then the judgment will come, Lord."

Realizing what he had said, Finney left the law office and ran out into the woods under deep conviction. Through repentance and faith Finney was born again.[3]

Henry Louis Gehrig, better known as "Lou" Gehrig, was one of America's greatest professional baseball players. Born in 1903, he died in 1941. Gehrig played 2130 consecutive games in fourteen seasons with the New York Yankees.

Roy Angell has a magnificent story in his book *Baskets of Silver* about

Lou Gehrig. Every preacher ought to have the story in his files.

Angell quotes a sportswriter for a New York newspaper: "Lou Gehrig came to bat with two out in the ninth inning. The winning runs were on second and third. New York was one run behind and the hit meant a win. The count on Lou Gehrig went to three balls and two strikes. The grandstand was in an uproar. The pitcher wound up deliberately and the third strike came smoking in straight over the middle of the plate and the umpire called 'Strike three,' for Lou Gehrig hadn't moved his bat. Very slowly Lou turned and spoke to the umpire. At this the crowd went wild, for no one had ever heard Lou Gehrig argue with an umpire. We reporters all piled over the seats and right out onto the field. We swarmed around the umpire. 'What did Lou Gehrig say to you?' we all asked in one breath. Whatever it was would make headlines on the sport page.

"The umpire smiled and yelled to Lou Gehrig to come over. 'Lou,' he said, 'tell the boys what you said to me when I called that third strike on you.'

"Lou looked a little bewildered as he answered, 'Mister Ump, I only said, I would give ten dollars to have that one back.'

"The reporter was so impressed that when he wrote up the story, he added, 'There are people all over the world who would give ten dollars or ten thousand dollars to get just one minute back and for the privilege of changing something they said or did in that minute.' "[4]

Praise be to God that He is the God of the second chance. This is what the new birth is all about.

Louise Fletcher Tarkington writes about beginning again like this:

> I wish there were some wonderful place
> In the Land of Beginning Again
> Where all our mistakes and all our heartaches
> And all of our poor selfish grief
> Could be dropped like a shabby old coat at the door
> And never put on again.

1. Hy. Pickering, *Twice Born Men* (London, Glasgow, Manchester, and Edinburgh: Pickering and Inglis, no date given), 120.

2. Ibid, 121.

3. James E. Hightower Jr., *Illustrating Paul's Letter To The Romans* (Nashville: Broadman Press, 1984), 49.

4. Roy Angell, *Baskets of Silver* (Nashville: Broadman Press, 1955), 35-36.

Burdens

For we that are in this tabernacle do groan, being burdened (2 Cor. 5:4).

Often there are blessings built into our burdens.

Nathaniel Hawthorne wrote and published *Twice-told Tales*. Still he could not live on the royalties they earned. Getting a job in the Salem, Mass., custom house, Hawthorne was paid one-hundred dollars a month, but a political change in Washington got Hawthorne dismissed from his job. Then another change brought him back. And another one put him out again!

But Hawthorne's experiences in the custom-house position played a very important role in his life and in American literature as well. The custom-house experience led to Hawthorne's publishing *The Scarlet Letter* in 1850 and instant recognition. Edward Fitzgerald described Hawthorne as "the most of a man of genius America has produced in the way of imagination." But for years Hawthorne was the obscurest man of letters in America. Had it not been for his burdens and hardships, Hawthorne would never have amounted to much.

There is a great university near San Francisco named after the son of a former governor of California. Leland Stanford University is one of America's finest.

Stanford was both governor of California and a United States senator. He founded the California university and named it after his son in 1885.

The Stanfords had only one son and the parents wanted the very best for him. To broaden his outlook on life, they took him to Italy when he was very young and he died there at the age of nine. Stanford and his wife returned to California brokenhearted. Although they had plenty of money, including a million-dollar house, nothing would satisfy them. After the death of their son, they felt they had nothing for which to live.

In a dream one night, Stanford said his son appeared to him and said: "Father, never say again that you have nothing to live for. Live for humanity, live for other people's children."

Stanford immediately awakened his wife and told her: "The only thing to do is to make all the children of California our children." So they built and endowed Leland Stanford University so that other young people might have the education and quality of life that death denied their son.[1]

One of the Scottish clans has for its motto, "Sub Pondere Cresco." The Latin words mean: "I grow under the burden."

Negro educator Booker T. Washington often spoke of "the advantages of disadvantages." And Helen Keller, the blind inspirationalist, said, "I thank God for my handicaps, for through them I have found myself, my work, and my God."

Everybody carries some kind of burden. How we handle our burdens will determine how we handle life.

John Milton was blind but he wrote *Paradise Lost*. Beethoven was deaf but he continued to create deathless music. Thomas A. Edison, the most gifted inventor of history, was almost totally deaf. William Booth, the founder of the Salvation Army, had to leave the Methodist Church in order to do what he felt God wanted him to do in the slums of east London. Author Sir Walter Scott and poet Lord Byron were both lame. Dr. George Washington Carver was the illegitimate son of a slave mother, but he became one of the greatest scientists in America's history. Abraham Lincoln had almost no formal schooling, but look at his accomplishments. Louis Pasteur had a club foot and suffered from a stroke in his later years, but he developed the process of medical immunization that has saved millions of lives.

Either we will handle our burdens or be handled by them. The choice is up to us.

We are not here to play, to dream and drift,

> We have work to do and loads to lift,
> Shun not the struggle, face it, 'tis God's gift.[2]

1. Henry Alford Porter, *Toward The Sunrising* (Nashville: Broadman Press, 1947), 43-44.
2. Author unknown.

Careful / Anxious

Be careful (anxious—NIV) for nothing (Phil. 4:6).

Herbert V. Prochnow says the Greek that is here translated "careful" in the King James, or "anxious" in the *New International Version,* comes from a word that means, "to be drawn in two direction," or "to be pulled apart, trying to do two things at the same time."[1]

Anxiety—which is closely akin to despair or depression—has plagued some of the best known people of history.

Abraham Lincoln wrestled with it all his life. Students of Lincoln know about his visions of his coffin guarded by soldiers in the White House. His days were full of melancholy.

Winston Churchill, England's great wartime prime minister, often spoke of the "black dog" of depression.

Painter Vincent Van Gogh, who in his early years was a Catholic priest, cut off one of his ears during an anxious time in his life.

Reformation catalyst Martin Luther said that anxiety or despair brought him "close to the gates of death and hell . . . shaken by desperation and blasphemy of God."[2]

Catherine Bowen in her biography of Justice Oliver Wendell Holmes, relates that Justice Holmes was looking for a book one day but it wasn't where he thought it ought to be. He made quite a scene, used some inappropriate language, and berated his wife because the book couldn't be found.

That evening when the justice returned from court the book was in its place on the shelf. Above it was a small United States flag and beneath the book was a sign Mrs. Holmes had printed: "I am a very old man. I have many troubles, most of which never happen."[3]

Thomas Carlyle (1795-1881), was a Scottish writer. Perhaps he is best remembered for his massive work *The French Revolution*.

At his home in Chelsea in London, visitors can still see Carlyle's soundproof study he had built so that the noise would not hinder his concentration.

But one of Carlyle's neighbors had a rooster and he crowed several times during the night. Carlyle complained to the owner who replied that his rooster seldom crowed more than twice in a night.

"That's just it," Carlyle responded. "I cannot tell you how I suffer waiting for him to crow!"

Most things about which we are prone to worry don't materialize after all. But, oh, how anxious we become waiting for those things to happen that never happen!

> Some of your hurts you have cured,
> And the sharpest you still have survived,
> But what torment of grief you endured
> From the evils which never arrived.
>
> —Ralph Waldo Emerson

1. Herbert V. Prochnow, *Speaker's Sourcebook of Stories, Illustrations, Epigrams and Quotations* (Grand Rapids, Mich.: Baker Book House, 1955), 77.

2. A. Dudley Dennison Jr., M. D., *Windows, Ladders, and Bridges* (Grand Rapids, Mich.: Zondervan Publishing House, 1976), 59.

3. Nenien C. McPherson Jr., *The Power Of A Purpose* (Westwood, N.J.: Fleming H. Revell Co., 1959), 24.

Church

. . . Christ also loved the church, and gave himself for it (Eph. 5:25).

The late Dr. J. D. Grey, who was pastor in New Orleans many years, liked to tell about the "lamest" excuse he ever heard for not attending church.

He said two deacons—or stewards if you are telling the story to Methodists—were out possum hunting one Wednesday night. While they were sitting under a tree waiting for a shower to pass, one of the deacons said to the other one, "This is Wednesday night and we ought to be at prayer meeting."

His friend replied: "It is Wednesday night isn't it? Well, we might as well be here. My wife is sick and I couldn't have gone anyway."[1]

Former Dallas Baptist University President W. E. Thorn tells about the poor brother who was stone deaf but attended church faithfully. He could be counted on to be there at every service. When someone asked the man why he went to church so regularly since he couldn't hear a thing that went on, the man replied, "To show my loyalty and to let others know where I stand."

The late author Roy Angell relates that during World War II, some American soldiers had been left behind to keep order in a small European town that had been retaken from the enemy.

The soldiers didn't have much to do to occupy their time so they decided to help the villagers restore their bombed-out homes and church. The soldiers first started to work on the church. It had taken a direct hit and was in terrible shape, but cheerfully they worked cleaning up the debris and putting things back in order.

One day as they were working, the soldiers found a marble statue of Jesus in the midst of the debris. It was badly broken and the hands of the statue were missing. And though the soldiers searched carefully, the hands could not be found.

They cemented the body of the statue together and stood it up in the church were it had once stood, but Jesus had no hands. One soldier, inspired by the handless Savior, made a sign and hung it on the statue: "He has no hands but yours."

Is it not our work to be the hands of Jesus to a lost world?[2]

Arthur Rubinstein was a great Polish-American pianist. At the age of twelve he was a soloist with the Berlin Symphony Orchestra. One of his teachers was the great Ignace Paderewski.

One Sunday when Rubinstein was visiting New York City, his host asked Rubinstein if he would like to attend church.

"Yes," the great pianist answered. "But I would like to go hear a preacher who will challenge me to do the impossible."[3]

Rudyard Kipling, the author, and William Booth, the founder of the Salvation Army, both received honorary degrees from Oxford University on the same day. As Booth and Kipling walked across the university quadrangle, Booth put to Kipling the most important question of all: "Young feller, how's your soul?"

That's the question Jesus told the church to keep asking the world.

In her book *Devotion For Personal and Group Worship*, Virginia Ely asks the question, "What if we had no hymns to sing except those produced by members of one religious group?"

Ely continues: "It was the Hebrews who gave us the Psalms; a Catholic who gave us "Lead, Kindly Light"; a Lutheran who gave us "A Mighty Fortress Is Our God"; a Methodist who gave us "Jesus, Lover of My Soul"; a Presbyterian who gave us "Jesus, Saviour, Pilot Me"; a Congregationalist who gave us "My Faith Looks Up to Thee"; a member of the Church of Scotland who gave us "O Love That Will Not Let Me Go"; and a Baptist who wrote:

Blest be the tie that binds
Our hearts in Christian love;
The fellowship of kindred minds
Is like to that above."[4]

One of America's great churches is Grace Baptist Church of Philadelphia. Dr. Russell H. Conwell, the author of *Acres of Diamonds*, founded both the church and Temple University. During the height of his ministry, Conwell preached to more than 4,000 people at the Sunday morning worship service.

But how the church, which was once called Baptist Temple, came to be built is not a well-known story.

Hattie Wyatt was a little girl who went to Sunday School in the old building which was located behind the current church building. One particular Sunday when she went to Sunday School she couldn't get in because there were too many children who wanted to go to Sunday School and the building was already full.

Little Hattie went home disappointed but determined to do something about the problem. She began to save her pennies so a church building large enough for everyone could be built.

Hattie saved until she had fifty-seven cents and then she became terminally ill. One day after she had died, her brokenhearted mother took the fifty-seven cents to Conwell and told him that Hattie had been saving for a new church building. Conwell was deeply moved and shared Hattie's vision with the congregation the next Sunday.

And the Lord used that fifty-seven cents. It became the seed-money for the raising of many thousands of dollars to build Grace Baptist Church. While the great building was being built people called it "Conwell's folly," but they quit calling it that when it was finished and filled to capacity week after week.

But that's still not all the story. From Grace Baptist Church came Temple University with its colleges of liberal arts, education, business, music, and fine arts. It has graduate programs in many fields including law, medicine, dentistry, pharmacy, and medical technology. Its students number in the thousands and its graduates in the tens of thousands.

The church and the university all owe their beginning to Hattie Wyatt and her fifty-seven cents.[5]

Don't Stay Away From Church

Because you are poor. There is no admission charge.

Because you are rich. We can help cure that.

Because it rains. You go to work in the rain.

Because it is hot. It's hot at your house, too.

Because it is cold. It's warm and friendly inside.

Because no one invited you. People go to the movies without being begged.

Because you have little children. What if you didn't have them any longer? We have a well-supervised nursery.

Because you don't like the preacher. He's human like you.

Because your job makes you tired. You may lose your job.

Because there are hypocrites. You associate with them daily.

Because you have company. They will admire your loyalty if you bring them along. Or tell them to wait until you get back.

Because you need a little weekend vacation occasionally. If your soul takes a vacation from God, it's not good.

Because your clothes are not expensive. Our church isn't supposed to be a fashion show anyway.

Because our church standard is too high. Take a look at the Bible standard if you think ours is high!

Because the church always wants money. So does your grocer.

—Author Unknown

1. J. D. Grey, *Epitaphs For Eager Preachers* (Nashville: Broadman Press, 1972), 72.

2. Roy Angell, *Baskets of Silver* (Nashville: Broadman Press, 1955), 18.

3. James P. Westberry, *When Hell Trembles and Other Sermons For Revivals* (Grand Rapids, Mich.: Baker Book House, 1974), 23.

4. Virginia Ely, *Devotion For Personal and Group Worship* (Westwood, N. J.: Fleming H. Revell, 1960), 109. Used by permission.

5. Clarence W. Cranford, *His Life Our Pattern* (Nashville: Broadman Press, 1950), 53-54.

Cross

And Pilate wrote a title, and put it on the cross. And the writing was,
JESUS OF NAZARETH THE KING OF THE JEWS (John 19:19).

R. C. Campbell wrote:

An ancient historian tells us that at the siege of Babylon, Darius condemned three thousand captives of war to death on the cross. Another
relates how Alexander inflicted long threatened vengeance on Tyre. He
crucified two thousand prisoners, and the crosses stood on her bloody
shores thicker than ships' masts in her crowded harbor. And when the
Romans let fly their eagles against Jerusalem, Titus, measuring out to the
Jews the measure they had meted out to Jesus, gave them crosses enough.
A spectator of the scenes, amid which Judah's sun set in blood forever,
tells us that wood was wanting for crosses, and crosses were wanting for
bodies. Yet, had Babylon's, Tyre's, or Jerusalem's crosses been raised to
save you, and on each cross of that forest, not a mere man but a dying angel
hung; had all heaven been crucified—all could not have revealed the love,
the compassion, the power, the comprehension of the Cross of Christ.[1]

Arkansas minister Randall O'Brien said that a fourteen-foot bronze
crucifix was stolen from Calvary Cemetery in Little Rock sometime between Dec. 9-14, 1988. The cross had stood at the entrance to the cemetery for more than half a century. The thieves apparently backed a large
truck up to the crucifix, tied a rope around it, took it off at its base, and
hauled it away.

Irene Bell, who managed the cemetery, reported that the cross cost
$10,000 when it was donated in 1930 by the late Catholic Bishop John B.
Morriss. Today the crucifix is reported to be worth $50,000—five times

more than it was when it was erected sixty years ago. But the cemetery has only offered a $1,000 reward for the cross's return.

Perhaps the cross was cut up into small pieces and sold as scrap metal for fifty cents a pound. Police believe that the 900-pound cross probably brought only about $450.

What is the cross worth to God the Father? What did it cost Jesus? What is the cross worth to you?

The late R. G. Lee wrote that Christ's crucifixion is mentioned in every book of the New Testament except Philemon, 2 John, and 3 John.

Lee wrote that Matthew mentioned the crucifixion in 141 verses; Mark gave 116 verses to the crucifixion; Luke devoted two long chapters to Christ's arrest and crucifixion; and John used half his gospel to deal with the events immediately preceding the crucifixion.

In Acts, Lee continued, everything centers around the cross: Peter at Pentecost spoke about Jesus crucified, and in the temple he spoke about their having "killed the Prince of life" (Acts 3:15); the apostles, arrested and brought before the authorities, spoke of "Jesus, whom ye slew and hanged on a tree" (Acts 5:30); and Cornelius was told about Jesus whom "God raised up the third day" (Acts 10:40).

At Antioch, Paul spoke of the suffering of Jesus (Acts 13:28-29); at Thessalonica, Paul preached "that it behoved Christ to suffer" (Luke 24:46; Acts 17:13); at Athens, Paul preached the death and resurrection of Jesus (Acts 17:31).[2]

Lee declared:

> Take the cross out of our preaching—whether that preaching be in tent or crude tabernacle or the isolated church up the creek or the country church or the big church in the city—is like taking heat out of fire, melody out of music, numbers out of mathematics, fact out of history, mind out of metaphysics, words out of vocabularies.[3]

An artist once painted a most unusual painting of Jesus on the cross. The background is dark, but the body of Jesus can clearly be seen. Gazing at the painting, one sees a second figure beginning to emerge from the shadows on the canvas. Behind the suffering Savior is the Heavenly Father. And the nails that pierce the hands and feet of Jesus also pierce the hands and feet of the Father. A crown of thorns that cuts into the brow of Jesus, cuts into the brow of the Father also. It is as if the artist is reminding us of Paul's statement: "God commendeth his love toward us, in that, while we were yet sinners, Christ died for us"(see Rom. 5:8).[4]

James Hefley relates that in 1910 another man named Jesus gave his life for his friends. His name was Jesus Garcia and he lived in Sonora, Mexico. As a young man, Jesus worked for the Montezuma Copper Company as a railroad fireman. Then he was promoted to engineer.

Jesus was at the train station in Nacozari, Sonora, one day when a fellow worker came running toward him and screaming that a train loaded with dynamite had caught fire on the tracks.

Without thinking about himself, Jesus ran toward the train realizing that unless something was done many people would die in the explosion. He reached the engine and headed the burning train out of town when it exploded, killing him instantly.

Hefley says Jesus Garcia is known as "the hero of Nacozari," and several streets have been named after him in the town. He is also memorialized by a street in Mexico City.[5]

But if a thousand Jesuses should die for us, it would avail nothing for our forgiveness and eternal salvation unless the death, burial, and resurrection of Jesus Christ is accepted in faith by us to atone for our sins.

Hungarian painter Michael Munkacsky's (1846-1900) painting of *Christ on Calvary* is a huge, magnificent painting twenty by thirty feet. It took Munkacsky three years to complete. On the very hill of Calvary, with the turrets and domes of Jerusalem visible in the distance, one's attention focuses on three crosses. The penitent thief hangs on Christ's right and his agonized face is turned pleadingly toward the Savior. The impenitent thief, whose head is sagging on his bosom, is on Christ's left.

Around the cross are Mary, Jesus' mother, weeping upon the feet of Jesus which she embraces. Mary Magdalene stands nearby with both hands covering her face. The other Mary lifts her left hand toward Jesus and with her uplifted right hand she begs the executioner to have mercy.

John, stunned and staring straight ahead, looks hopeless. A young man with outstretched hands stands at the center listening to Christ pray for his persecutors. And the high priest with his long white beard lifts his left hand and shouts derisively, "Let the Christ, the King of Israel, come down from the cross that we may see and believe."

The centurion, on his horse, looks at the Savior with the look of faith. The sun is darkened and Christ is dying.

But no matter from what angle one looks at Munkacsky's picture of the crucifixion, Jesus is the central figure. With mouth half open, he is crying, "My God, My God, why have You forsaken Me?"

In telling the story of Munkacsky's painting, Thomas J. Villers in his book *The Hurry Call of Jesus*, says that a young sailor from Toronto, Canada, was viewing the picture one day with tears streaming down his cheeks.

As he reverently tiptoed away, he said to the old caretaker: "My mother told me that story often when I was a little boy, but I never believed it. I see now that it is all true and that Christ died for all of us and especially for me. Today I have accepted him as my Savior."[6]

1. R. C. Campbell, *The Christ of The Centuries* (Nashville: Broadman Press, 1947), 13-14.

2. Robert G. Lee, *The Must of The Second Birth* (Westwood, N. J.: Fleming H. Revell, 1959), 10-12.

3. Ibid., 12.

4. A. Dudley Dennison Jr., *Windows, Ladders, and Bridges* (Grand Rapids, Mich.: Zondervan Publishing House, 1976), 92.

5. James C. Hefley, *Dictionary of Illustrations* (Grand Rapids, Mich.: Zondervan Publishing House, 1971), 45.

6. Thomas Jefferson Villers, *The Hurry Call of Jesus* (Boston and Chicago: Judson Press, 1927), 275-278.

Death

Death is swallowed up in victory (1 Cor. 15:54).

The great Michaelangelo lived to be eighty-nine. When he was well along in years, he and a friend were discussing death. "After such a good life, it's hard to look death in the eye," the friend said.

"Not at all!" replied Michaelangelo. "Since life was such a pleasure, death coming from the great Source cannot displease us."[1]

John Wesley, the founder of Methodism, died on March 2, 1791. On the day before he died, Wesley said with the little strength he had left, "The best of all is, God is with us!"[2]

After a long journey in January's bitter cold, Martin Luther died in 1546. Justice Jonas who was with Luther when he died, sensing the end was near, asked: "Reverend Father, wilt thou stand by Christ and the doctrine thou hast preached?"

Luther responded with a single word: "Yes."

Polycarp, born about A.D. 65(?), was the bishop of Smyrna. Polycarp lived during that first-century period when some believers who had known Jesus were still alive, and Polycarp had known some of them.

Arrested in A.D. 155 at Smyrna, Polycarp went to meet those who had come to arrest him. He offered them something to eat and then asked that he might have an hour to pray.

When he was brought before the city prefect, Polycarp was asked: "What harm is there in saying, Lord Caesar, and then sacrificing with the other ceremonies observed on such occasions, and so make sure of safety?" But Polycarp replied, "I shall not do as you advise."

When they brought Polycarp into the arena, the proconsul demanded that Polycarp "Swear by the fortune of Caesar; repent, and reproach Christ."

But Polycarp answered: "Eighty and six years have I served him, and he never did me any injury; how then can I blaspheme my King and my Savior?"

Pressed again by the proconsul to "Swear by the fortune of Caesar," Polycarp replied: "Since you are vainly urgent that, as you say, I should swear by the fortune of Caesar, and pretend not to know who and what I am, hear me declare with boldness, I am a Christian."

The proconsul had a herald proclaim to the large crowd assembled that, "Polycarp has confessed that he is a Christian."

"This is the teacher of Asia, the father of Christians, and the over-thrower of our Gods, he who has been teaching many not to sacrifice to or to worship the Gods."

The people clamored for Polycarp to be thrown to the lions, but the proconsul replied that the shows that included the wild beasts were over.

"Let him be burnt, then," the wild throng demanded. So, binding Polycarp to a stake, they piled fagots around him and lighted the flames.

Polycarp's last utterance was: "O Lord God Almighty, the Father of thy beloved and blessed son Jesus Christ, by whom we have received the knowledge of thee, the God of angels and powers and of every creature, and of the whole race of the righteous who live before thee, I give thee thanks that thou hast counted me worthy of this day and hour, that I should have a part in the number of thy martyrs, in the cup of Christ."[3]

Death is a debt that all must pay. Sooner or later we are dealt "the dead man's hand" and we must play it.

This expression, "the dead man's hand," originated on August 2, 1876. James Butler Hickok, better known as "Wild Bill Hickok," rode into Deadwood, South Dakota, in June 1876 with the notorious Calamity Jane.

On August 2, 1876, "Wild Bill" sat down at a poker table in Deadwood's saloon Number 10. Jack McCall entered the saloon and shot Bill through the head. In "Wild Bill's" hand when he died were two pairs—

aces and eights. The combination has been known ever since as "the dead man's hand."[4] It's a hand we must all play.

Knowing that he must play "the dead man's hand," King Philip of Macedon, the father of Alexander the Great, assigned a strange duty to one of his slaves. The slave was instructed by the king to come each morning into his presence and say: "Remember, Philip, thou must die." The slave was told to let nothing interfere with his making that important announcement each day.

1. Jacob M. Braude, *Braude's Handbook of Stories for Toastmasters and Speakers* (Englewood Cliffs, N. J.: Prentice-Hall Inc., 1957), 210. Used by permission.

2. Author's personal file, see Death #37.

3. Walter Russell Bowie, *Men of Fire: Torchbearers of the Gospel* (New York: Harper & Row Publishers, 1961), 23-25.

4. David Wallechinsky and Irving Wallace, *People's Almanac* (Garden City, N. Y.: Doubleday and Co., Inc., 1975), 99.

Example

Be thou an example of the believers (1 Tim. 4:12).

The life of David Brainerd, a missionary to the American Indians, was a great influence on Henry Martyn, a distinguished student at Cambridge who gave his life in missionary service to India. Brainerd's holy life was also a prime factor inspiring William Carey to become a missionary to India.

It was Carey's life, in turn, that inspired Adoniram Judson, who, along with his wife Ann, went to India as America's first missionaries.

Robert H. Glover in his book *The Progress of Worldwide Missions*, wrote:

> And so we trace the spiritual lineage from step to step—Huss, Wycliffe, Francke, Zinzendorf, the Wesleys and Whitefield, Brainerd, Edwards, Carey, Judson, and ever onward in the true apostolic succession of spiritual grace and power and worldwide ministry.[1]

It was the example of a fellow apprentice who worked in a shoe cobbler's shop by the side of William Carey that helped lead Carey to the Savior. Carey said about his young friend: "He could not answer my questions, but I could not answer his life." What the example of the young man meant to Christendom will not be told until eternity's books are opened. Carey, born of poor parents in the small village of North Hamptonshire, England, in 1761, died on June 9, 1834, and entered into his eternal rest. He had served Christ in India forty-one years.

Think of the influence of Carey's shoe cobbler friend. He could not answer Carey's questions, but Carey could not answer his life.

Example   **53**

And what did Carey leave behind in India? In an article printed in 1969 titled, "What India Owes to Christianity," a review is given: 150 colleges, 2,177 high schools, 214 technical schools, and 153 teachers' training schools.

Also, Christianity had given to India, up until 1969, 620 hospitals, 670 dispensaries, 86 leprosy centers, 713 orphanages, 87 homes for the aged, 681 hostels and welfare organizations—and this only begins to tell the story.[2]

Probably the greatest preacher since apostolic days was Charles Haddon Spurgeon of England (1834-1892).

In her book *Devotion For Personal and Group Worship*, Virginia Ely tells a story about Spurgeon's frequent visits to Monaco, one of the smallest states in Europe and located on the northeastern end of the French Riviera. It has been a gambling resort for many years.

Spurgeon, of course, was not a gambler, but he enjoyed visiting the grounds of the Casino of Monte Carlo and walking through its lavish gardens. Spurgeon thought the gardens there were some of the most beautiful in the world. One day after a conversation with a friend, Spurgeon determined that he would never visit the beautiful gardens of the Casino of Monte Carlo again.

The owner of one of the gambling houses had said to Spurgeon's friend, "You hardly ever visit my gardens anymore."

Spurgeon's friend replied that since he didn't gamble it would not be fair of him to continue to enjoy the beautiful gardens without making some contribution to the casino.

But Monsieur Blanc, the casino owner, encouraged the friend to continue visiting the gardens because Blanc would lose customers in his gambling house if the friend quit visiting the gardens.

"There are many people who don't intend to gamble in the casino," Blanc said, "who feel quite comfortable visiting the gardens. Then, from the gardens," Blanc continued, "it is but a short distance to the gambling tables. You see, when you visit my gardens, respectable person that you are, you attract other people who eventually become my gambling customers."

The story relates that after Spurgeon heard about this he never went near the gardens of Monte Carlo again. He knew that his example was too important.[3]

1. Robert H. Glover, *The Progress of Worldwide Missions* (New York and London: Harper & Row Publishers, 1953), 88. Used by permission.

2. Donald T. Kauffman, *For Instance* (Grand Rapids, Mich.: Baker Book House, 1972), 51.

3. Virginia Ely, *Devotion For Personal and Group Worship* (Westwood, N. J. Fleming H. Revell, 1960), 78-79.

Faith

If you have faith as a grain of mustard seed (Matt. 17:20).

George Muller was a man of great faith. He founded Great Britain's orphanage ministry.

An 1825 graduate of the University of Halle, Muller was more interested in women, drinking, and worldly pleasures as a university student than he was in his studies. His interest in Christianity was almost nonexistent. But God was working in Muller's life and he began to ponder the faith promises of Jesus in the Gospels. "Did Jesus really mean what he said about 'asking'?" Muller wondered.

Sitting in his room one day looking out over the town to the sea beyond, Muller thought about people he knew who were afraid of life or afraid to launch out on some daring, life-changing vocation.

As he thought about the faith-promises of Jesus and people whose lives were empty and drab, he saw walking on the cobblestone sidewalk below two little orphan girls who had no one to care for them. Their father had gone down with his ship in the Magellan Straits and only two weeks before their mother had died of tuberculosis. Knowing the girls, Muller was aware that the eleven and thirteen-year-old girls had three younger brothers and sisters at home for whom they were trying to care. "What will happen to them?" Muller questioned.

Mueller turned to an open Bible lying on the table beside him. Suddenly from the Scriptures, God spoke to Muller: "Open thy mouth wide and I will fill it" (Psalm 81:10). Bowing his head, Muller said he was opening his mouth to ask for divine guidance and he made the promise to do what the Lord wanted him to do.

In 1830 he married Mary Groves and they determined to part with all their worldly goods and depend on God alone for their support. They gave away their possessions, not telling a soul why they were doing it.

Muller opened his first orphan's home on April 21, 1836, in a rented building. Within days, they had forty-three children for whom to care. Among the commitments Muller and his fellow workers made to God were these: They would never solicit funds, never incur debts, and their financial accounts would be audited annually.

Continuing to pray for God's blessings and depending upon him to supply those blessings, Muller's work grew by leaps and bounds. Starting out with forty-three children in a rented building, they eventually had five new buildings, 110 co-workers, and 2,050 orphans.

Before Muller opened his first rented building to orphans he told the Heavenly Father that the experiment would be counted a failure if a child went a day without food in the orphanage.

God blessed remarkably. The children were not taken care of minimally, but had maximum provisions: three pairs of shoes each; three suits for each boy; and five dresses for each girl. In addition, the tables were always covered with white tablecloths for the evening meal and flowers were on the table when in season.

For more than sixty years, as George Muller recorded in his "Journals," God miraculously blessed George and Mary's faith. It was such a testimony to God's willingness to provide for his people that when Muller was seventy he began to travel, sharing God's blessings on the ministry with believers in forty-two countries.[1]

Muller's life was an undeniable testimony to how God blesses faith.

The largest seminary in the world is Southwestern Baptist Theological Seminary which is located in Fort Worth, Texas. Originally founded in Waco, Texas, in 1908, the seminary was relocated in Fort Worth in 1910. The founder and first president of the seminary was Dr. B. H. Carroll.

Southwestern Seminary's Robert A. Baker, professor emeritus of church history, tells about the vision of faith Carroll had as he rode a train passing through the Texas Panhandle in the spring of 1905.

"As I looked out over those plains over which in my youth I had chased the buffalo there arose before me a vision of our Baptist situation in the Southwest. I saw multitudes of our preachers with very limited education, with few books and with small skill in using to the best advantage even the books they had.

"I saw here in the Southwest many institutions for the professional training of the young teacher, the young lawyer, the young doctor, the young nurse and the young farmer, but not a single institution dedicated to the specific training of the young Baptist preacher. It weighed upon my soul like the earth on the shoulder of Atlas.

"It was made clear to me on that memorable day that, for the highest usefulness of our Baptist people, such an institution was an imperious necessity. I seemed to hear the age-old question of God: 'Whom shall I send and who will go for me?'

"I . . . was about to dismiss the matter, feeling that I could not do it—when there came to me as clearly as if audibly spoken the assuring word of our Lord: 'I am he that liveth, and was dead, and behold, I am alive for evermore.'

"When I came to myself I was standing gripping the back of the seat in front of me. Becoming conscious that my fellow passengers were looking at me, some with amusement and some with amazement, I sat down, confused, embarrassed, and humiliated. But from that hour I knew as definitely as I ever knew anything, that God would plant a great school here in the Southwest for the training of our young Baptist preachers."[2]

By faith Carroll planted the seeds that grew into the largest seminary in the world. Since its founding, the seminary has enrolled 51,082 students and graduated 27,249. For more than eighty years these students have served Christ at home and abroad.

1. Catherine Marshall, *Beyond Ourselves* (New York: McGraw-Hill, Inc., 1961), 74-79.

2. Robert A. Baker, *Tell The Generations Following* (Nashville: Broadman Press, 1983), 24-25.

Fear

Do not be afraid. I am the First and the Last (Rev. 1:17, NIV).

The late Harry Emerson Fosdick told an interesting story about Edward R. Murrow, one of the best-known news commentators of the 20th century.

Murrow said that in 1940 when Nazi bombers were bombing London each night, he saw a crudely lettered sign on a church that said: "If your knees knock, kneel on them."[1]

There is an old Arabian story that Charles Wellborn relates in his book *This Is the Hour.*

A traveler once saw a hideous looking figure outside the gates of an ancient city. As they met they spoke, and the traveler asked, "What is your name?"

"My name is Pestilence," the hideous-looking stranger replied.

"And where are you going?" asked the traveling man.

"I am going to the city," Pestilence replied.

"And what are you going to do there?" asked the traveler.

"I am going to take 5,000 lives," Pestilence stated.

Sometime later the two met again, this time outside the gates of another city.

"The last time we met you did not tell me the truth," the traveling man said. "Fifty thousand people died in my city, but you said you were only going to take the lives of 5,000 people."

"But I did tell you the truth," Pestilence replied. "I took the lives of only 5,000 people. The other 45,000 died from fear."[2]

Nenien C. McPherson, Jr., says that the fear of falling and the fear of loud noises are the only fears that are natural to us. There are only two, he says, and all the rest are learned. McPherson then quotes well-known psychiatrist Dr. William Sadler who said that "the only known cure (for fear) is faith."[3]

Dr. Norman Vincent Peale gives nine steps to overcoming fear in his book *The Amazing Results of Positive Thinking*: (1) Pinpoint your fears. (2) Understand why you are afraid. (3) Get your fear out into the open. (4) Fill your mind with faith. (5) Do your very best. (6) Stand up to your fears. (7) Pray through your fears. (8) Affirm the sufficient grace of God in your fears. (9) God is with you even when you are afraid.[4]

Our English word *phobia* comes from the Greek word *phobos*. A Phobia is an irrational, excessive fear of something. It is out-of-control fear.

Author J. Wallace Hamilton says that a good dictionary will contain more than seventy-five phobias. Some of these better-known phobias are acrophobia—fear of heights; claustrophobia—fear of closed places; agoraphobia—fear of open places; neophobia—fear of the new; pathophobia—fear of disease; photophobia—fear of lights; spermaphobia—fear of germs; ergophobia—fear of work; ereuthophobia—fear of blushing; and phobophobia—fear of everything.[5]

But for all our fears and phobias, Jesus has just the right word, "Fear not" (Rev. 1:17).

1. Harry Emerson Fosdick, *What Is Vital in Religion*, 9.

2. Charles Wellborn, *This Is the Hour*, 52.

3. Nenien C. McPherson, Jr., *The Power of Our Purpose* (Old Tappan, N. J.: Fleming H. Revell Co., 1969), 37.

4. Norman Vincent Peale, *The Amazing Results of Positive Thinking* (Englewood Cliffs, N. J.: Prentice Hall Inc., 1959), 134-135.

5. J. Wallace Hamilton, *Ride the Wild Horses* (Old Tappan, N. J.: Fleming H. Revell Co., 1952), 105.

Forgiveness

In whom we have redemption through his blood, the forgiveness of sins (Eph. 1:7).

A. J. Cronin was a British doctor who gave up the practice of medicine to write such novels as *The Keys of the Kingdom*, *Hatters' Castle*, and *The Spanish Gardener*. A surgeon during World War I, he studied medicine at the University of Glasgow, Scotland, and moved to the United States after World War II.

Roy Angell, in his book *Iron Shoes*, relates an interesting and well-known story about Cronin.

Cronin's first assignment after finishing medical school was in a Welsh town and his first operation was a tracheotomy. A little girl with a severe case of diphtheria was brought to Cronin and the doctor discovered that her throat was filled with membrane. After Cronin had made a small incision in the girl's windpipe with his scalpel, he put the tube in the windpipe and watched as the brightness of life came back to the little girl's face.

Cronin's nurse was a nineteen-year-old country girl who had just finished her training. Exhausted from his day of work, Cronin decided about midnight that he would sleep for a little while and he asked his young nurse, "Do you think you can take care of the little girl for a while and let me get some sleep?"

When the nurse assured the doctor that she could take care of things, Cronin told her what to do: "The tube may get stopped up. You might have to take it out and clean it, then put it back in quickly. You will have plenty of time to do it. Then, come and call me," Cronin told her.

After Cronin had gone to sleep, the tube did get stopped up and the nurse panicked. Rather than removing the tube and cleaning it as Cronin had instructed her, she ran to the doctor and waked him, urging him to come quickly. But by the time the doctor got to the little girl, it was too late.

Cronin said he was furious at the nurse for what she had done. For twenty minutes he exploded at her and the next morning he wrote a long letter to her superiors telling them why the young nurse's license should be taken away and why it should never have been granted in the first place. Calling the nurse in, Cronin read the letter to her and told her that he was going to send it to the board and have her license revoked.

Cronin said: "I looked at her as she sat there with her face down, chin against her chest, and a little pity stirred in my heart as she raised her face and looked at me pathetically and pleaded, 'Doctor, give me one more chance.' The tears were awfully close to running down her cheeks, her eyes were full. I turned away and laid the letter down. 'I'll think about it,' I told her. All night long in my dreams there came that same quiet, pleading little voice, 'Give me one more chance,' and I waked up and prayed, 'O Jesus, that's what I had to ask you to do one day, Give me one more chance. O God forgive me for what I nearly did.' "[1]

Many years after that incident, Cronin said that the nurse was then superintendent of the largest children's hospital in all Great Britain.

Sir Wilfred Grenfell (1865-1849) was a British medical missionary to Labrador. The late Baptist minister C. Roy Angell knew Dr. Grenfell and asked him one day, when both of them lived in England, what influenced Grenfell to give his life so unreservedly to God. Here is Grenfell's reply as it was retold by R. L. Middleton in his book *The Gift of Love*:

> Into the hospital where I was a resident physician, a woman terribly burned was brought one night. We all saw immediately that there was not hope for her. We discovered that her husband came home drunk and threw a paraffin [kerosene] lamp over her.
>
> We summoned the police, and when they arrived, they brought with them the half-sobered husband. The magistrate leaned over the bed and insisted that the patient tell the police exactly what happened. He tried to

impress upon her the importance of telling the exact truth since she had only an hour to live. She turned her face from side to side, avoiding looking at her husband who stood at the foot of the bed, a miserable creature.

Finally, her eyes came to rest on his hands and slowly raised to his face. The look of suffering disappeared from her face and in its place there came one of tenderness, love, and all the beautiful things that a woman's face can express. She looked back then to the magistrate and said in a quiet clear voice: "Sir, it was just an accident." With a shadow of a smile still on her face, she snuggled down in the pillows and died."

Dr. Grenfell said that he went back to his room and sat for a long time on his bed in meditation. "Finally," he said, "I spoke out loud. That was like God, and God is like that. His love sees through our sins." There is no greater love in the world than God's love for His children.[2]

1. C. Roy Angell, *Iron Shoes* (Nashville: Broadman Press, 1953), 35.
2. R. L. Middleton, *The Gift of Love* (Nashville: Broadman Press, 1976), 35-36.

Foundation

He is like a man which built an house, and digged deep, and laid the foundation on a rock (Luke 6:48),

Dr. Norman Vincent Peale relates that most of New York City's Manhattan Island is solid bedrock. Because of that foundation, scores of towering skyscrapers have been built on Manhattan.

But when builders started digging for the foundation for the Chase Manhattan Bank, they ran into trouble. Unlike much of the area, the excavators knew before they started digging that the site was not solid rock. But they were not prepared to find oozy quicksand.

Knowing that no building could be erected on such an undependable foundation, the bankers called in the experts. One suggested driving pilings deep into the quicksand until a solid base was hit. Another said they should seal the quicksand off with watertight caissons. But the cost of using either method was prohibitive.

They called in some geologists. "How long will it take to turn this quicksand into solid rock?" they asked. The geologists responded, about a million years. The bankers felt they couldn't wait that long!

The solution was finally found when some experts dealing with that particular problem were summoned. Sinking pipes into the quicksand, they pumped in sodium salicylate and calcium chloride. In only a few days the quicksand hardened. Soon the foundation was laid and the sixty-floor bank building was erected on the solid foundation.[1]

1. Norman Vincent Peale, *The Amazing Results of Positive Thinking* (Englewood Cliffs, N. J.: Prentice-Hall, Inc., 1959), 10.

God

There is one God (Jas. 2:19).

The late Helen Keller whose sight and hearing were destroyed by an illness before she was two years of age, was a great woman.

Anne Sullivan who lived with Keller and taught her for many years thought it would be impossible to teach little Helen about God. But when Helen was fourteen, she placed her sensitive fingers on the throat and lips of Miss Sullivan as Sullivan slowly said "G-O-D."

It was a breakthrough. Helen's face lighted up and she exclaimed: "Oh, I am so glad you told me His name, for He has often spoken to me."[1]

What are His names? Elohim—great, mighty; El Shaddai—God Almighty; Adonai—Owner, ruler, Lord; Jehovah—most commonly used name in the Old Testament—means the One who is, was, and will be.

He is also called Jehovah-Tsidkenu (Jer. 23:5-6)—our righteousness; Jehovah-M/Kaddesh (Lev. 20:7)—the One who sanctifies; Shalom (Judg. 6:24)—our peace; Jehovah-Jireh (Gen. 22:14)—the provider; Jehovah-Rophene (Ex. 15:26)—healer; Jehovah-Nissi (Ex. 17:15)—our banner; Jehovah-Rohi (Ps. 23:1)—shepherd; and Jehovah-Shammah (Ezek. 48:35)—the One who is there.[2]

But all His blessed names are summed up in the name Jesus Christ. The late R. G. Lee often said: "Jesus is as much God as God is God and as much man as man is man." He is the full, final and total revelation of almighty God.

Wayne Dehoney in his book *Challenges To The Cross*, says that hundreds of birds die each night beating their wings against the light and the upraised arm of Miss Liberty in New York Harbor. Each morning the caretakers gather up hundreds of these broken little bodies scattered around the base of the statue, but the light still shines. And those who say there is no God, like those little birds in their futile pursuit, only destroy themselves in attacking Him.

The fourth-century church father Augustine said there is a God blank in us which only God can fill. "Give me Thine own self, without which, though Thou shouldest give all that ever Thou hadst made, yet could not my desire be satisfied," Augustine prayed.

A biographer of St. Francis of Assisi (1181-1226) wrote that St. Francis prayed all night on one occasion uttering at intervals but one word: "God . . . God . . . God."

Years ago $48,000 was left the Royal Society of Great Britain to investigate and then demonstrate conclusively the existence of God. Twelve volumes were produced as evidence. But the existence of God is proved not in the test tubes of the scientists or by the spade of the archaeologist, but by the experience of the human heart.

In his book *Seven Reasons Why A Scientist Believes in God*, Cressya A. Morrison gives these seven reasons:

1) The rotation of the earth—it rotates on its axis at about one thousand miles an hour. If it were faster or slower our earth would burn up or freeze in a day or a night.

2) The heat of the sun—with a surface temperature of 12,000 degrees Fahrenheit, the sun is close enough yet far enough away sufficiently to warm us. If it emitted only half its current heat, we would freeze. If it gave half as much more than it does, the earth would have been reduced to ashes millennia ago.

3) The tilt of the earth—tilted at an angle of 23 degrees, it gives us our seasons. If the earth were not tilted, the North and South poles would be in eternal twilight and water vapor from the ocean would move North and South piling up continents of ice and leaving between them vast de-

serts. If the tilt were not right, oceans would be lowered and rainfall on all parts of the earth would be diminished with terrible results.

4) The regulation of the tides—if all the air of the earth were liquefied, the earth would be covered with thirty-five feet of water. The moon is 240,000 miles away and twice a day the tides rise and fall because of the moon. If the moon were closer, the tides would be enormous and destroy twice a day all the lowlands of the earth. If the continents were then washed away, the average depth of water over the whole earth would be one and one-half miles and life could not exist.

5) The symmetery of creation—if the crust of the earth were 10 feet thicker, there would be no oxygen and animal and plant life could not live. If the atmosphere were thinner, meteors that now burn out in the atmosphere would strike the earth by the millions every day. Traveling from six to forty miles a second, these fiery meteors would set fire to everything combustible on the earth.

6) The fact of life—created life—plant, animal, man—gives evidence of a divine Creator. Life did not just "happen."

7) The fact of animal wisdom—Morrison cites the bee, the spider, the salmon, etc. and the way they live and the marvelous things they do as evidence for the existence of a divine Creator.[3]

1. G.B.F. Hallock, *5,000 Thousand Best Modern Illustrations* (New York: George H. Doran Co., 1927), 317.

2. Fowler's file, First Baptist Church, Albuquerque, NM, Bulletin.

3. Cressy A. Morrison, *Seven Reasons Why A Scientist Believes in God*, 12-13, Fowler's file.

Grace

For by grace are ye saved through faith; and that not of yourselves: it is the gift of God (Eph. 2:8).

The late Moody Bible Institute Greek scholar Kenneth Wuest defined "grace" as "a favor freely done, without claim or expectation of return."[1]

Wuest further declared that in pagan Greece this favor was always done for a friend, never an enemy. But in the New Testament, he said, it takes an infinite leap forward, it takes on a meaning it never had in pagan Greece. God's saving grace expressed at the cross is targeted at those who are His enemies (see Rom. 5:10).

Earle V. Pierce tells how studying the grace of God affected evangelist Dwight L. Moody.

Moody loved to study the Bible topically and it occurred to him one day that he had never studied the subject of grace. Setting aside a day, Moody gave himself to the study of God's grace.

But a second day was required, and even on the third day Moody had not finished his task.

By the late afternoon of the third day, however, Moody was so filled with his subject that he had to go out on the street and talk to somebody about it. Stopping a complete stranger, Moody said, "My friend, do you know anything about grace?"

Surprised at the question, the man replied, "Grace who?"

"Why," Moody responded, "the grace of God that brings salvation." Moody then left the stranger standing on the street considering the good news of the grace of God.[2]

Sam Jones was a well-known Methodist evangelist. Born in Alabama in 1847, Jones died in Oklahoma in 1906 during an evangelistic campaign.

Jones's mother died while he was young and his godly grandmother was a great influence on his life. She was of such a devout nature that she read the Bible through thirty-seven times on her knees.

Sam's father was a lawyer and when the Union army marched through Georgia, the family fled into Kentucky. There Sam Jones married and began to drink—a habit he continued for ten years.

Admitted to the Georgia bar in 1869, Jones's drinking kept him from being a success in the legal profession. But in 1872, Sam's life took a radical turn. His father died that year and his dying words stirred Sam deeply: "My poor, wicked, wayward, reckless boy. You have broken the heart of your sweet wife and brought me down in sorrow to my grave; promise me, my boy, to meet me in heaven."[3]

Sam, who was in his mid-twenties, made the solemn vow to his father that he would quit drinking and meet him in heaven.

Jones kept his word. He became a Christian and almost immediately surrendered to preach. One week after his conversion, he preached his first sermon.

Sam Jones was a great trophy of the grace of God.

Henry Wadsworth Longfellow could write a poem and it would be worth hundreds of dollars. We call that talent.

John Jacob Astor could sign his name to a piece of paper and buy a skyscraper. We call that capital.

The United States Treasury Department can take a special piece of paper and some special ink, press it between special plates and make a $100 bill. We call that money.

The Wright Brothers could take some used bicycle parts, wire, metal and canvas covering and make an airplane. We call that genius.

Michaelangelo could take some brushes and some paints and paint a masterpiece on the ceiling of the Sistine Chapel. We call that art.

A mechanic can take a used and ruined part from your automobile engine, replace it with a new one, and make the car nearly as good as new. We call that skill.

And God can take a poor worthless, devastated hell-bound sinner, wash him in the blood of Jesus Christ, place his Holy Spirit in him, and create a brand new person (see 2 Cor. 5:17). We call that grace.

During the nineteenth century when evangelist Dwight L. Moody was at his zenith, a notorious burglar by the name of Valentine Burke was arrested and jailed in St. Louis.

One day Burke's cellmate was reading a newspaper and the headlines, "Jailer At Philippi Caught," grabbed Burke's attention. Burke borrowed the paper and read the article only to discover that it was an account of Dwight Moody's sermon on the Philippian jailer preached the night before in the city. In the newspaper account of the sermon, Burke read again and again the oft-repeated words of Acts 16:31: "Believe on the Lord Jesus Christ, and thou shalt be saved." And there in the jail cell that day Burke was saved.

Moody later visited Valentine Burke in New York City where he was serving as a deputy sheriff.

Burke had been entrusted as a deputy to guard some precious jewels and he told Moody about it. Showing Moody the jewels, Burke said: "Look, they trust me to guard them. See what the grace of God has done for a burglar."[4]

1. Kenneth S. Wuest, *The Pastoral Epistles in the Greek New Testament* (Grand Rapids, Mich.: William B. Eerdmans Publishing Co., 1954), 193.

2. Earle V. Pierce, *The Supreme Beatitude* (New York, London, and Edinburgh: Fleming H. Revell Co., 1947), 100.

3. Clyde E. Fant Jr. and William M. Pinson Jr., *20 Centuries Of Great Preaching, Vol. VI* (Dallas, Texas: Word Books Inc., 1971), 324. Used by permission.

4. Walter B. Knight, *Knights Master Book of New Illustrations* (Grand Rapids, Mich., William B. Eerdmans Publishing Co., 1956), 259.

Heaven

For we know that if our earthly house of this tabernacle were dissolved, we have a building of God, an house not made with hands, eternal in the heavens (2 Cor. 5:1).

In his book *Man In Black*, singer Johnny Cash tells about the death of his brother Jack in 1944.

The family lived in Arkansas and times were hard. Jack was working on Saturdays cutting fence posts and cleaning up around the school's agricultural building earning three dollars each Saturday.

Johnny wanted to go fishing and asked Jack to go, but Jack refused saying he needed to earn the three dollars. About noon, the preacher and Johnny's father drove up in an A-model Ford and told Johnny to get in, that Jack had been seriously injured in an accident.

When they got back to the house, Johnny learned that Jack had been pulled into the large saw he was using and that his condition was very grave. Dr. Hollingsworth, the family doctor, told the family there was no chance that Jack could live.

Several days passed and Jack lapsed into and out of a coma. Hallucinating, Jack would be plowing with the mules and yelling at them, and then he would be quiet for a while.

The following Sunday morning the family gathered in Jack's room because they knew he couldn't live much longer. Mrs. Cash sat on the bed and held Jack's hand. Dr. Hollingsworth was praying: "Lord, I've done everything a doctor can do. It's out of my hands. Only You can save him."

Mr. and Mrs. Cash got down on their knees to pray and Johnny bent over Jack, put his cheek against Jack's cheek, and said, "Goodbye, Jack."

At 6:30 AM Jack came out of his coma. Looking around the room, he asked, "Why is everybody crying over me? Mama, don't cry over me. Did you see the river?"

"No, Jack," his mother answered, "I didn't see it, Son."

Still talking to his mother, he told her that he "was going toward the fire," but was now headed in the other direction. "I was going down a river, and there was fire on one side and heaven on the other. I was crying, 'God, I'm supposed to go to heaven. Don't you remember?' And all of the sudden I turned. Mama, can you hear the angels singing?"

But Mrs. Cash said she couldn't hear the angels. Squeezing her hand, Jack said, "But Mama, you've got to hear them." And as the tears rolled down Jack's cheeks, he said to his mother, "Listen to the angels. I am going there, Mama."

"What a beautiful city," he said. "And the angels singing. Oh, Mama, I wish you could hear the angels singing."

And Johnny Cash said those were Jack's last words.[1]

The great American evangelist Dwight L. Moody is buried at Northfield, Massachusetts. Moody's son, Will, related that as his father lay on his deathbed almost unconscious, his face suddenly lighted up and he cried out, "Dwight! Irene! I can see the children's faces!" Dwight was a grandson and Irene was a granddaughter. Each had died within a year of the other.[2]

Dr. C. Roy Angell tells about the death of his friend Ben Bronner who had been confined to a wheelchair for about two years. His condition was so deteriorated that he even had to sleep in the wheelchair.

Mrs. Bronner called Dr. Angell and told him that Ben wanted the pastor to come to the Bronner home. And although it was midnight, Dr. Angell went.

When Angell arrived at the house, Bronner was asleep but in a few minutes he awakened, recognized his pastor, and said "Good news, Roy, I'm going home before the day is over and I'm so glad."

Addressing his wife, Bronner told her to bring all his fishing gear in and when she did he gave it to Dr. Angell.

"Remember the good times we had fishing, Roy?" he asked. "After I'm gone, take the fishing gear and enjoy it. Don't let it rust. Use it and wear it out and think of me when you catch a big one."

Angell said he was shocked by Bronner's next question.

"Didn't your father die recently?" Bronner asked. When Angell replied that his father had died the previous December, Bronner asked if Angell would like to send a message to him. "I think I'll know him when I see him over there," Bronner said.

Bronner then instructed the pastor: "Take my body down to the old burying ground in Virginia, the old home burial ground, and bury it. . . . And tell the folks Ben Bronner was smiling when he went home."[3]

Beulah Carroll Orrick is my sister-in-law who is well along in years. As a child, her family lived in McCullough County, Texas. Her grandfather and grandmother, Andy and Mary Metts, lived in Coleman County, Texas, thirty-five miles away.

According to Mrs. Orrick, Grandma Metts was never very well. During her last illness, she had been unconscious for some time and had neither spoken nor moved day or night. The grown-ups took turns sitting silently by Grandma's bed and the little children, with sad hearts, puzzled over Grandma's condition.

Mrs. Orrick said: "Then it happened. My sister, Lurlene, and I were standing at the foot of the old iron bed just looking at Grandma when suddenly she stirred. A bright smile came to her face. She raised her right arm, full-length, pointed upward and said loudly enough that everyone heard, 'Oh, look!'

"Of course, everyone in the room looked up. Then Grandma said, 'See Jesus! Ain't He pretty!'

"Her hand fell limply to her chest and she was gone—gone to be with the 'pretty,' sweet Jesus whom we all know she loved so much.

"For a time there was shocked silence. No one moved except to look up to try to see what Grandma saw. Then there were sobs of release, relief, and joy. There was no doubt in anyone's mind where Grandma was," Mrs. Orrick said.

That's what Jesus said He would do. He promised to come for us:

"And if I go and prepare a place for you, I will come again and receive you unto myself; that where I am, there ye may be also" (John 14:3).

Monument Avenue in Richmond, Virginia, is lined with the monuments of Confederate heroes. Two of the most striking, magnificent monuments are to the memories of Confederate Generals Robert E. Lee and Stonewall Jackson.

Not too long ago, I stood before the Stonewall Jackson monument and remembered his last words: "Let us cross over the river and rest under the shade of the trees."

Born in Virginia in 1824, Jackson distinguished himself in the first Battle of Bull Run. Facing overwhelming Yankee odds at Bull Run (Manassas, Va.), on July 21, 1861, Jackson's men held their position in the midst of a hail of bullets.

Trying to rally his Confederate troops in the heat of the battle, General Barnard E. Bee saw Jackson and his men holding the line of battle and Bee shouted to his weary troops, "There is Jackson standing like a stone wall. Let us determine to die here, and we will conquer."[4]

The name stuck. And from that time on, Jackson was known as "Stonewall."

Jackson was greatly loved by his men. One observer said Jackson's men would "meet death for his sake, and bless him when dying."[5]

A graduate of the United States Military Academy at West Point, Jackson graduated in the upper third of his class. It was no little accomplishment for Jackson whose academic preparation was inadequate, and who had to work much harder to keep up than did the other cadets. But he was a determined student—a determination that made him a gallant soldier and leader of men in the Civil War.

Jackson's greatest battle was fought in May 1863. Meeting the troops of Yankee General Joseph Hooker near Chancellorsville, Virginia, Jackson routed the Yankees. As night fell, Jackson went out ahead of his line to survey his situation. Tragically, one of his own men mistook him for a Yankee soldier and shot him.

The doctors tried to save Jackson's life by amputating his left arm, but to no avail. When Lee was told of Jackson's mortal wounds, he replied:

"He has lost his left arm, but I have lost my right arm." Eight days later, on May 10, Stonewall Jackson died.

It was a Sunday—clear and pleasant. Jackson, a devout Christian, often had said he wanted to die on Sunday. And God granted Jackson's wish.

A soldier to the end, Jackson, apparently, was refighting old battles toward the end. Suddenly, he spoke in his delirium: "Order A. P. Hill to prepare for action! Pass the infantry to the front! Tell Major Hawks . . ."[6]

For a while he was silent. At 3:15 PM Jackson's delirium cleared and in a normal voice he said: "Let us cross over the river and rest under the shade of the trees."[7]

And with those simple words of faith, one of the South's noblest sons died.

1. Johnny Cash, *Man In Black* (Grand Rapids, Mich.: Zondervan, 1975).

2. John Sutherland Bonnell, *I Believe In Immortality* (New York and Nashville: Abingdon Press, 1959), 68.

3. Roy Angell, *Iron Shoes* (Nashville: Broadman Press, 1953), 108-109.

4. *Encyclopedia Britanica*, in loco.

5. Ibid, 15.

6. Philip Van Doren Stern, *Robert E. Lee, The Man and The Soldier* (New York: Bonanza Books, 1963), 174.

7. Ibid, 174.

Hell

And in hell he lift up his eyes, being in torments (Luke 16:23).

The word *hell* is used glibly and frequently today by worldlings. It is one of their choice and most-used curse words. But how little do they know the tragedy and grief bound up in the word they use so glibly.

1. A lake of fire (Rev. 20:15);
2. A bottomless pit (Rev. 20:1);
3. A horrible tempest (Ps. 11:6);
4. Everlasting burnings (Isa. 33:14);
5. A furnace of fire (Matt. 13:41-42);
6. A devouring fire (Isa. 33:14);
7. A prison (2 Peter 2:4);
8. A place of torments (Luke 16:23);
9. A place of everlasting punishment (Matt. 25:46);
10. A place where people pray (Luke 16:27);
11. A place where they scream for mercy (Luke 16:24);
12. A place where they wail (Matt. 13:42);
13. A place where they curse God (Rev. 16:11);
14. A place where they can never repent (Matt. 12:32);
15. A place of weeping (Matt. 8:12);
16. A place of sorrows (Ps. 18:5);
17. A place of outer darkness (Matt. 8:12);
18. A place where they have no rest (Rev. 14:11);
19. A place of blackness or darkness forever (Jude 13);
20. A place where their worm dieth not, and the fire is not quenched (Mark 9:48);

21. A place of fiery torment (Luke 16:24);

22. A place where the lost drink the wine of the wrath of God. (Rev. 14:10);

23. A place where no lost sinner will want his/her loved ones to come (Luke 16:28);

24. A place prepared for the devil and his angels (Matt. 25:41);

25. A place where there are dogs, sorcerers, and whoremongers (Rev. 22:15);

26. A place where there are murderers liars, fearful and abominable (Rev. 21:8); and

27. A storm of burning coals of fire (Ps. 11:6).

No one need go to hell for Christ came to seek and to save the lost (Luke 19:10).[1]

The great English missionary C. T. Studd said:

> Some want to live within the sound
> of church or chapel bell.
> I want to run a rescue shop
> Within a yard of Hell.

Amos Kendall was postmaster general of the United States under both Presidents Andrew Jackson and Martin Van Buren.

Although he was not a Christian, Kendall gave a considerable sum of money to help build the Calvary Baptist Church in Washington, D. C. He gave the money on the condition that the church would receive into its membership not only those who came on profession of their faith in Jesus Christ as their Savior, presenting themselves for baptism, but also it would receive into membership those who only promised to contribute regularly to the work of the church, relates the late Clarence Cranford.

After he had joined the church on the latter condition, a woman visited Kendall one day and told him that her son had died without accepting Christ as his Savior. She then shocked Kendall with the statement that if her son was eternally lost and had gone to hell, it was Kendall's fault. "Every time someone talked to my son about accepting Christ, he would always reply that Amos Kendall is a good man who did not need to become a professing Christian. 'So why should I?' " the grieving mother told Kendall the boy had asked.

Kendall was so moved that, as an old man, he became a Christian and was baptized into the fellowship of Washington's E Street Baptist Church.[2]

1. Author Unknown.
2. Clarence W. Cranford, *His Life Our Pattern* (Nashville: Broadman Press, Nashville, 1960), 111-112.

Home

Go home to thy friends (Mark 5:19).

The home was the first institution created by God. And it is under a great attack today. By the time you read these statistics they will be out-of-date: six million incidents of serious family abuse occur annually, 25 percent of all murders are among family members, child abuse is a national scandal, 100,000-plus elementary school children drink on a weekly basis, alcohol-related accidents are the chief cause of death among young people and suicide is next. And more children under five die of injuries inflicted by parents than from all common childhood diseases combined.

How much different things would be if fathers and mothers were Christians, treated their children as Jesus teaches, and built their homes on Christian principles.

Scottish author Thomas Carlyle (1795-1881) was born in Ecclefechan, Scotland. Norman Vincent Peale says that Carlyle "started off to Edinburgh for his education with a schilling in his pocket and he walked into immortality."

Ecclefechan is located halfway between the Scottish border and the small town of Dumfries. They were special places to Carlyle and he could have been buried in London's great Westminster Abbey, but he chose to be buried in his hometown cemetery at Ecclefechan.

Once Queen Victoria asked Carlyle what he considered to be the most beautiful road in Great Britain and Carlyle answered, "Why, Your Majesty, it is the road from Ecclefechan to Dumfries."

When the much-loved queen asked Carlyle what he considered to be the second most beautiful road in Great Britain, Carlyle replied, "Why, it's the road back to Ecclefechan."[1]

What was he saying? He was simply saying that the road home is the most beautiful road in the world. It doesn't matter if home is a palatial building by the side of a beautiful lake, a vine-covered cottage in the woods, or a shack by the side of the railroad tracks. Although we don't recognize it in youth, the most beautiful road in the world is the road that leads back home.

I guess that's what Salty the dog was thinking when he made his 300-mile trek back home.

In September 1971, Margie LaBeff and her little daughter gave Salty to a family who lived in Cheboygan, Michigan, 300 miles from Detroit where the LaBeffs live. They felt Salty needed some room to run and play, but by December Salty was read to go home.

Salty got back to Detroit, a 300-mile trip through the snowy cold of a Michigan winter. She was wet, tired, sore of foot, and almost unrecognizable. Mrs. LaBeff said Salty was so wet, tired and dirty that it was difficult for them to tell she was the once well-groomed black and white dog who had lived at their house. She had almost starved to death. But Salty finally got back home.[2]

I guess Salty believed there is no place like home!

Roy Angell wrote that several years ago 600 university students were asked to write on a piece of paper the one word in the English language which they considered to be the most beautiful. Four hundred and twenty-two wrote the word *mother*, and 112 wrote *home*.[3]

Some of history's greatest personalities have come from large families. George Washington, our first president, was one of ten children; William Shakespeare, the great writer, was one of eight children; Benjamin Franklin, inventor and politician, was the tenth child in a family of thirteen children; the great Methodist preacher John Wesley had twenty brothers and sisters; Phillips Brooks, the respected Boston pastor and author of "O Little Town of Bethlehem," was one of nine children; Lyman Beecher, Presbyterian and Congregationalist minister and the father of Harriet Beecher Stowe who wrote the anti-slavery novel *Uncle Tom's Cabin*, was one of thirteen children; and England's greatest poet, Alfred Tennyson, was one twelve children.[4]

Jack Gulledge relates that a Kentucky man and his wife were in the process of getting a divorce. When he received a summons one day to appear to settle the disposition of their property, he drew a line through the middle of their house labeling one side "his" and the other "hers." Taking a chain saw, he sawed the house in half.[5]

But half a house does not a happy home make!

American novelist and short-story writer F. Scott Fitzgerald (1896-1940) was the author of *The Great Gatsby* and *The Last Tycoon*. The latter was called the best novel ever written about Hollywood.

Roy Angell relates that the day Fitzgerald died he was working on a new novel about a wealthy man who dies and leaves his millions to his relatives. But there was a catch to it. To receive the money, the relatives had to come and live together in the benefactor's spacious mansion.

Fitzgerald had only outlined the plot of the novel when death took him away unexpectedly. Below the outline of the plot were scribbled the words, "This could be a little spot of hell."[6]

True, but home can also be a little spot of heaven.

1. Norman Vincent Peale, *The Amazing Results of Positive Thinking* (Englewood Cliffs, N. J.: Prentice-Hall Inc., 1959), 9.

2. *Proclaim* Magazine, July 1980.

3. Roy Angell, *Rejoicing On Great Days* (Nashville: Broadman Press, 1968), 43.

4. Benjamin P. Browne, *Illustrations for Preaching* (Nashville: Broadman Press, 1977), 98-99.

5. Jack Gulledge, *Ideas and Illustrations for Inspirational Talks* (Nashville: Broadman Press, 1986), 53.

6. Roy Angell, *Shields of Brass* (Nashville: Broadman Press, 1965), 26.

Honesty

. . . Lead a quiet and peaceable life in all godliness and honesty (1 Tim. 2:2).

One of the greatest Christian gentlemen who ever lived was General Robert E. Lee. An Episcopalian, Lee was a son of old Virginia, the leader of the Confederate forces in the Civil War, and honest to a fault.

In 1845, when Lee was stationed at Fort Hamilton, New York, a mistake was made and Lee drew his pay twice for May and June. The error was caught by a clerk in Washington and a letter was sent to Lee asking for an explanation.

Lee had not noticed the error. So when he received the clerk's letter, he quickly refunded the duplicate payment and no charges where filed against Lee.

Lee then wrote a letter to the adjutant general in which he offered a humble apology: "I am gratified to find that you believe me incapable of intentionally committing this act; I assure you that it has caused me more mortification than any other act of my life to find that I have been culpably negligent when the strictest accuracy is both necessary and required."[1]

General Ulysses S. Grant, leader of the Union forces during the war, was also an honest man.

After Grant left the presidency, he found himself deeply in debt. A fall from his horse kept him indoors for some time and unprincipled business partners plunged the ex-president deeply into debt. Oftentimes, Grant had to depend upon the good will of his friends just to get by.

But during those difficult days Grant set about writing his memoirs to pay off his debts. He determined to write the story of the great war, in which he had fought, and leave his family with a good name.

Grant had not gone very far in writing his memoirs, however, when his final sickness overtook him. But propped up in a chair at his McGregor, New York, home, Grant wrote on even as his throat cancer progressed.

Four days before his death Grant wrote: "I feel that we are on the eve of a new era, where there is to be great harmony between Confederate and Federal. I cannot stay to be a living witness to the correctness of this philosophy; but I feel it within me that it is to be so."[2]

Clarence Macartney, the great Presbyterian minister who last served First Presbyterian Church, Pittsburgh, Penn., wrote about this gallant act of Grant: "That was Grant's greatest victory."

Perhaps all your life you have heard about George Washington cutting down the cherry tree. Well, here are the facts behind that story.

The story was written by Mason Weems, an American clergyman, who was born in 1760 and died in 1825. The cherry tree story appears in Weems' *Life of George Washington; with Curious Anecdotes, Equally Honorable to Himself, and Exemplary to his Young Countrymen.*

It must be added, however, that some believe "Parson" Weems had a flair for exaggeration.

Weems wrote:

> When George was about 6 years old, he was made the wealthy owner of a hatchet! of which, like most little boys, he was immoderately fond; and was constantly going about chopping every thing which came in his way. One day, in the garden, where he often amused himself by hacking his mother's pea-sticks, he unluckily tried the edge of his hatchet on the body of a beautiful young English cherry tree, which he barked so terribly, that I don't believe the tree ever got the better of it. The next morning, the old gentleman, finding out what had befallen his tree, which, by the by, was a great favourite, came into the house; and with much warmth asked for the mischievous author, declaring at the same time, that he would not have taken 5 guineas for his tree. Nobody would tell him anything about it. Presently George and his hatchet made their appearance. "George," said his father, "do you know who killed that beautiful little cherry tree yonder in the garden?"

This was a tough question; and George staggered under it for a moment; but quickly recovered himself; and looking at his father, with the sweet face of youth brightened with the inexpressible charm of all-conquering truth, he bravely cried out, "I can't tell a lie, Pa; you know I can't tell a lie. I did cut it with my hatchet."—"Run to my arms you dearest boy," cried his father in transports, "run to my arms; glad am I, George, that you killed my tree, for you have paid me for it a thousand fold. Such an act of heroism in my son is worth more than a thousand trees, though blossomed with silver and their fruits of purest gold."[3]

1. Philip Van Doren Stern, *Robert E. Lee, The Man and The Soldier* (New York: Bonanza Books, 1963), 71.

2. Clarence E. Macartney, *Macartney's Illustrations* (New York and Nashville: Abingdon-Cokesbury Press, 1945), 12.

3. David Wallechinsky and Irving Wallace, *The People's Almanac* (New York: Doubleday & Co, Inc., 1975), 114.

Hope

Rejoicing in hope (Rom. 12:12).

French scientists once experimented on a convict who had been convicted for murder and sentenced to death. The condemned man was strapped to a table and told that an artery in his arm was to be severed and that he would bleed to death in a matter of minutes.

The scientists proceeded with their experiment. They made only a superficial wound on the surface of the convict's skin, but they did not tell him how superficial it was. Then they poured warm water over his arm, which he thought was blood. In just a few minutes he died because he had been convinced of the hopelessness of his situation.[1]

Clarence Macartney tells that in London's Tate Gallery hangs the original painting of the familiar prints seen in the offices of so many physicians. The painting, titled, "The Doctor," was painted by L. Fields. The compassionate physician is sitting by the bed of a child in a humble home. The doctor's head is resting on his hand and his eyes are carefully watching his little sufferer. Beside the bed a lamp burns and medicine glasses and spoons are close by.

Nearby the mother sits at the table with her head resting on the table. Her face is buried in her arms. By her side stands the husband and his hand is resting on the shoulder of the grieving mother. The father's face is turned in hope toward the doctor, anticipating, waiting for some encouraging word.[2]

In his book *Success Through a Positive Mental Attitude*, Napoleon Hill tells about a successful cosmetic manufacturer who decided he would retire at the age of sixty-five. Each year thereafter, his friends and former business associates gave him a birthday party and tried to find out the "secret" for his special cosmetic formula. But year after year he refused, good-naturedly, to reveal his secret.

"Maybe I will tell you next year," he would say.

This went on for ten years until the man celebrated his seventy-fifth birthday. As usual, at his birthday party his former associates begged him to share the secret formula with them so they could continue the business after his death. Finally, he yielded to their insistence.

He confessed to his friends that they had treated him so wonderfully that he would now reveal his formula. "In addition to the things which I use which are commonly known," he said, "there is one secret ingredient that I package with every bottle."

By this time, everyone at the party was listening with rapt attention. The day had finally come when they were about to learn the "secret" of the magic formula.

"What is it?" an anxious friend inquired. "Please, don't keep us in suspense any longer."

The cosmetic manufacturer replied: "I never told a woman that my product would make her beautiful, but I always gave her hope."

"Hope," he said, "is the magic ingredient."[3]

Hope in Christ is shown in this story from Benjamin Browne.
Felix Mendelssohn (1809-1847) was a German composer. Although Mendelssohn's career was short, he wrote some significant and unforgettable music. He came from a prominent banking family and his musical talent became evident when he was quite young.

One day Mendelssohn went into the cathedral at Freiburg and asked if he could play the great organ. The caretaker, not knowing it was Felix Mendelssohn, rather abruptly denounced the stranger for his audacity and let him know in no uncertain way that strangers who came in off the street could certainly not play the priceless organ.

But Mendelssohn continued to insist that he be permitted to play, if ever so briefly. The caretaker continued to refuse, telling the stranger that only master musicians could play the cathedral's precious console.

But Mendelssohn insisted and finally convinced the caretaker.

Mendelssohn was told he could play one small tune on the organ and that was all. And to be sure that the stranger didn't overstep the bounds set by the caretaker, the old man went up to the organ and stood beside it while Mendelssohn played.

Mendelssohn began slowly, moving his trained, slender fingers over the keyboard ever so slowly and gently. And as he did, the instrument sighed sweetly under the master's strokes of love.

Mendelssohn played on and on and the old caretaker stood there with his mouth open and with his eyes lifted toward the heavens as the cathedral resounded with the sounds of the heavenly music. Never had the caretaker heard anything like that in all the years he had cared for the cathedral and its precious organ.

The organ thundered and shook the cathedral and the old caretaker wept as Mendelssohn played on and on. Then, when Mendelssohn had stopped, the caretaker who was barely able to speak said, "Tell me, sir, what is your name?"

"My name is Felix Mendelssohn," the great composer replied.

"Oh," the caretaker said barely audible. "Can you forgive a foolish old man? Never in all my life have I heard such beautiful, glorious and heavenly music. And to think, I nearly refused the master the opportunity to play on my organ. I nearly missed hearing the most beautiful music on earth or in heaven."

So, Christ, the Master and Almighty Musician, can stroke the strings of our soul and bring from deep within us melodies of hope and joy we never knew were there. With His presence, He can turn our sunsets into sunrises and our midnights into noonday.[4]

1. Source unknown (J. B. Fowler's personal file)

2. Clarence Macartney, *Macartney's Illustrations* (New York and Nashville: Abingdon-Cokesbury Press, 1945), 171.

3. Napoleon Hill, *Success Through a Positive Mental Attitude* (Englewood Cliffs, N. J.: Prentice-Hall Publishers, 1960), 102-103.

4. Benjamin P. Browne, *Illustrations For Preaching* (Nashville: Broadman Press, 1977), 30-31.

Humble/Humility

Humble yourselves therefore under the mighty hand of God (1 Pet. 5:6).

The late R. L. Middleton wrote that one fall day in 1943, two young women who were riding out in the Minnesota countryside saw a blood-mobile parked in front of a school building. Thinking it was an opportunity to give blood and help with a worthy cause, they pulled up in front.

As they entered the building, an elderly man dressed in coveralls was carrying a bucket of water down the corridor. Thinking he was probably the custodian, the ladies complimented him on the beautiful school saying they felt sure he enjoyed working there.

But he wasn't the custodian. He told the young ladies that he was a Greek and his country was at war and that this was really the only service he could render to help his country.

That night the ladies had tickets to hear the Minneapolis Symphony. As the program began a little gray-haired man came out on the platform, took his bow, and began to direct the symphony. The conductor was Dimitri Mitropoulos, a musician known throughout the world. And he was the same little man the ladies had seen carrying water earlier that day at the schoolhouse.

"Even though he had reached the peak of his musical career, he was humble enough to render a modest service for others in need. Humility is indeed a mark of greatness," Middleton wrote.[1]

In *Wellsprings of Wisdom*, Ralph L. Wood told about a student on summer vacation in Europe who visited the home of Beethoven. With the brashness of youth, she asked the caretaker for permission to play Beethoven's piano. After she had played a few bars of music on the priceless instrument, the student asked: "I'm sure that all the great musicians who visit this place play Beethoven's piano, don't they?"

"No, they don't," the caretaker replied. "All the great pianists have been here but none of them has ever played Beethoven's piano because they felt unworthy. My experience is that the great people are the humblest. Perhaps that's what makes them great."[2]

In his book *The Burden of The Lord*, Ian Macpherson retold Joseph Parker's fable about the ambitious watch. Parker was a London contemporary of Charles Haddon Spurgeon.

According to Parker, there was once a beautiful watch suspended by a gold chain from the neck of a sophisticated lady. One day as the lady's carriage was crossing Westminster Bridge, the little watch looked up at Big Ben in his tower high above the Thames and said to himself, "Oh, if I could only be up there where Big Ben is everybody would see me and I would be so happy telling all the passers-by the time."

According to Parker's fable, the wish was granted. One day a very thin thread was attached to the little watch and it was carefully hoisted to the Parliament tower where Big Ben has chimed the hours for decades. But, the higher the little watch was hoisted, the harder it was for anybody to see it. Finally, when it was by the side of Big Ben, not a soul in London could see the watch and its life was very lonely because it was of no good to anyone."[3]

Stephen A. Douglas, United States congressman and senator from Illinois, was known as "the little giant" because he was short. But what Douglas lacked in size, he made up in brain power.

A history student well knows about the Abraham Lincoln and Stephen Douglas debates. Lincoln was opposed to the spread of slavery and Douglas, though he did not own slaves himself, was not opposed to slavery. When Douglas ran for re-election to the Senate in 1858, his Republican opponent was Abraham Lincoln and the Lincoln-Douglas debates were much the making of Lincoln.

When Lincoln was first inaugurated president on March 4, 1861, he was introduced by Oregon Senator E. D. Baker. In his hands Lincoln carried a cane and a small rolled-up manuscript of his inaugural address.

For a few minutes after Baker's introduction, there was an awkward pause while Lincoln looked around for a place to put his high silk hat.

Stephen A. Douglas, Lincoln's strong political opponent, was seated just behind Lincoln. Douglas arose, stepped forward quickly and took Lincoln's hat and held it until Lincoln finished his speech.

"If I can't be president, I can at least hold his hat," Douglas whispered to Mrs. Brown who was a cousin of Lincoln's.[4]

1. R. L. Middleton, *The Gift of Love* (Nashville: Broadman Press, 1976), 107.
2. Ralph L. Wood, *Wellsprings of Wisdom* (Norwalk, Conn.: The C. R. Gibbons Co., 1959), 15.
3. Ian Macpherson, *The Burden of the Lord* (New York and Nashville: Abingdon Press, 1955), 123-124.
4. G.B.F. Hallock, *5000 Best Modern Illustrations* (New York: George H. Doran Co., 1927), 445.

Idle/Idleness

He went out, and found others standing idle (Matt. 20:6).

Victorious Roman legions, left behind to rule a defeated Spain, built an aqueduct in Segovia in AD 109. And for 1,800 years—sixty generations—that aqueduct carried sparkling water to hot and dusty Segovians. About the turn of the twentieth century thoughtful Spaniards decided that the aqueduct should be preserved for posterity, and be relieved of its age-old labor.

They laid modern pipelines and stopped the flow that for years had gushed and gurgled in the aqueduct. Shortly thereafter the aqueduct began to fall apart! The blazing sun dried the mortar and made it crumble. Its stones sagged and fell and soon it lay in ruins.

What ages of use could not destroy, idleness rapidly did.[1]

Years ago, in an edition of *The Reader's Digest*, W. K. Welch told a story that, though undoubtedly fictitious, illustrates idleness (in this case maybe laziness is a better word).

Welch said he was spending the night with a Kentucky mountaineer and his nineteen-year-old son. They sat in front of the roaring fire crossing and uncrossing their legs and puffing on their corncob pipes. Conversation was scarce. After a long silence, the old man said to his son, "Boy, why don't you go outside and see if it's raining?"

The boy neither looked up nor moved. In a little bit he replied, "Paw, let's just call the dogs in and see if they're wet."[2]

1. Author unknown, (J. B. Fowler's personal file).
2. Jacob M. Braude, *Braude's Handbook of Stories for Toastmasters and Speakers* (Englewood Cliffs, N. J.: Prentice-Hall Inc., 1957), 204.

Immortality

. . . And this mortal must put on immortality (1 Cor. 15:53).

Immanuel Kant defined immortality as "the infinitely prolonged existence and personality of one and the same rational being." Christians believe that life continues after this life.

French poet and novelist Victor Hugo (1802-1885) wrote on his seventieth birthday:

> Winter is on my head, and eternal spring is in my heart. The nearer I approach the end, the plainer I hear around me the immortal symphonies of the worlds which invite me. . . . For half a century I have been writing my thoughts in prose, verse, history, philosophy, drama, romance, tradition, satire, ode, song—I have tried it all. But I feel that I have not said the thousandth part of what is in me.[1]

John Sutherland Bonnell wrote: "God did not build our minds to fit them merely into the brief and fleeting life of earth, for we are constantly thinking 'thoughts that wander through eternity.' "[2]

This life ends when the next one begins. Thomas Chalmers, called Scotland's greatest preacher, spoke a cheery farewell on Sunday evening as he retired. "I expect you to give worship in the morning," he said. And Chalmers did. In the Father's house.

When Abraham Lincoln's young son, Willie, died on February 20, 1862, Lincoln was plunged into deep despair and Mrs. Lincoln could not be consoled. Dr. Venton, pastor of Trinity Church, New York, came to the White House to comfort Lincoln in his uncontrollable grief.

"Your son is alive in paradise," Dr. Venton said.

The President had hardly heard a word the minister had said. Lincoln's ears seemed to be deaf to everything that was being said to comfort him until the four words, "Your son is alive" penetrated the darkness of Lincoln's mind. Jumping up from the sofa, he exclaimed, "Alive! Alive! Surely, you mock me."

"No, Sir, believe me," Dr. Venton said. "It is a most comforting doctrine of the church, founded upon the words of Christ Himself."

For some minutes Mr. Lincoln sobbed and repeated to himself, "Alive! Alive!"[3]

Robert Ingersoll (1833-1899) was an American lawyer and perhaps the best-known agnostic in his day. At his brother's funeral Ingersoll said: "From the voiceless lips of the unreplying dead there comes no word. But in the night of death, hope sees a star and listening love can hear the rustling of a wing."[4]

1. John Sutherland Bonnell, *I Believe In Immortality* (New York and Nashville: Abington Press, 1959), 13-14.

2. Ibid., 14.

3. Author unknown, (from J. B. Fowler's personal file).

4. Robert J. McCracken, *Putting Faith To Work* (New York: Harper & Brothers Publishers, 1960), 70.

Jealous/Jealousy

I am jealous over you (2 Cor. 11:2).

Ian Macpherson retold the old story of the destructive power of jealousy.

In an ancient legend, the devil was crossing the Libyan Desert one day when he came upon a holy man being harassed by a pack of demons.

Having no character of their own, they were trying to steal the character of the holy man. They were placing doubts and fears in his mind, tempting him with the lusts of the flesh, and telling him that his austere, sacrificial life was for nothing. But they were making no headway with the strong, old Christian.

Seeing their temptations were fruitless, the devil called his imps off to one side and told them they were going about it in the wrong way. "Let me try my hand at him," the devil said.

Approaching the old Christian, the devil said, "I guess you haven't heard the good news."

"What good news?" the hermit asked.

"Why," the devil replied, "Your brother has been made the bishop of Alexandria."

And with that, according to the fable, jealousy began to cloud the sweet countenance of the devout believer.[1]

The late R. G. Lee wrote: "Jealousy is essentially selfish. It calls for all successes, all compliments, all advantages, all accomplishments—everything to be for itself.

"Dr. Riley said: 'Let no man conclude that divine favor and God's use of a man will insure against human hatred. Jealousy is the blindest of passions. Jealousy never sees anything except through green glasses which convert all virtues into vice.' "

Lee continued:

> Because of jealousy, Cain slew Abel. Because of jealousy, Miriam criticized Moses. Because of jealousy, King Saul sought to slay David. Because of jealousy, Joseph's brethren sold him into slavery. Because of jealousy, Christ's enemies sent him to the cross.
>
> The havoc wrought by jealousy, no one can estimate. The story of jealousy between and among nations is written in letters of blood and fire across all the pages of history. Jealousy poisons our social relations, our political relations, our religious relations. And what a devastating despoiler it is of domestic relations. Daily, homes intended to be a foretaste of heaven are turned into vestibules of hell by the demon of jealousy. Jealousy is the scandal in the home of love. Because of jealousy's slaying of people— their peace of mind, their rectitude, their reputation—I could with gladness and gratitude conduct its funeral.[2]

Jealousy, according to the dictionary, is resentful suspicion of one's rival; it is a resentful enviousness. One author says it is "an unpleasant fear, suspicion or resentment, arising from mistrust of another."[3]

William Shakespeare defined jealousy as a "green-eyed monster." John Dryden said it is the "jaundice of the soul." And King Solomon wrote that "Love is as strong as death, (but) jealousy (is) as cruel as hell."

1. Ian Macpherson, *Live Sermon Outlines* (Grand Rapids, Mich.: Baker Book House, 1974), 36.

2. R. G. Lee, *The Must of the Second Birth* (Westwood, N. J.: Fleming H. Revell Co., 1959), 83.

3. Taken from A. Dudley Dennison, Jr., *Windows, Ladders, and Bridges* (Grand Rapids, Mich.: The Zondervan Corp., 1976). Used by permission.

Jesus / Christ

For the law was given by Moses, but grace and truth came by Jesus Christ (John 1:17).

One of the greatest artists of the Italian Renaissance was Leonardo da Vinci (1452-1519). "The Last Supper," a mural painted by da Vinci in the dining hall of the monastery of Santa Maria delle Grazie, in Milan is considered to be one of the greatest paintings in the world.

It is related that after da Vinci had finished "The Last Supper," he invited one of his artist friends to look at the painting and give his views.

After the painting was thoroughly examined by the artist, he said to da Vinci: "You have painted the chalice on the table with exquisite beauty. It is the most beautiful thing in the whole picture and captivates the eyes of the beholder."

Benjamin P. Browne, in *Illustrations for Preaching*, wrote that da Vinci picked up his palette and brush and with a few, masterful strokes removed the magnificent beautiful chalice from the painting.

When asked why he had done such a thing, da Vinci replied that he wanted nothing to take the viewer's attention away from Jesus. "It is the Christ who must be preeminently seen as the center of my painting," da Vinci replied.[1]

James Hefley discloses in *A Dictionary of Illustrations* that the *Encyclopedia Britannica*, in its discussion about Jesus Christ, uses a total of 20,000 words.

This is more words than the Britannica allows for Aristotle, Alexander the Great, Cicero, Julius Caesar, or Napoleon Bonaparte. H. G. Wells blasphemed Jesus, yet he felt compelled to discuss Jesus on 10 pages in his

Outline of History and never questioned that a man named Jesus did live.[2]

One Solitary Life

Here is a young man who was born in an obscure village, the child of a peasant woman. He grew up in another village. He worked in a carpenter shop until He was thirty, and then for three years He was an itinerant preacher. He never wrote a book. He never held an office. He never owned a home. He never had a family. He never went to college. He never put his foot inside a big city. He never traveled 200 miles from the place where He was born. He never did any one of the things that usually accompany greatness. He has no credentials but Himself.

While He was still a young man, the tide of public opinion turned against Him. His friends ran away. He was turned over to His enemies. He went through the mockery of a trial. He was nailed to a cross between two thieves. While He was dying, His executioners gambled for the only piece of property He had on earth and that was His coat.

When He was dead, He was laid in a borrowed grave through the pity of a friend.

Nineteen centuries have come and gone, and today He is the central figure of the human race and the leader of the column of progress.

I am far within the mark when I say that all the armies that ever marched, and all the navies that ever sailed, and all the parliaments that ever sat, and all the kings that ever reigned, put together, have not affected the life of man upon this earth as has that one solitary life.[3]

Lubbock, Texas, Baptist minister J. Ralph Grant, wrote:

The enemies of Christ have said that many great persons in the ancient world were reputed to be supernaturally born. They point to Buddha, Zoroaster, Pythagoras, and Plato, all of whom acquired weird stories about their origins. The Greeks had a fable that Perseus was born of a virgin and that Jupiter had come down in a shower of gold. There was the Hindu myth that claimed that Krishna was born of the virgin Davaki. Alexander the Great, the Greek warrior, did not want to be known as an ordinary son of Philip of Macedon; he claimed to have been begotten by a serpent. Around Caesar Augustus, the conqueror of the Roman world, there grew up the myth that while his mother lay asleep in the temple of Apollo, she conceived by a serpent and bore her famous son.

All these are meaningless myths, fables, fictitious folklore. But the virgin birth of the Lord Jesus Christ is a divine fact, and the world needs to rediscover this glorious reality, this good news[4] (see Matt. 1:18-20).

When evangelist Billy Graham visited American soldiers in Korea during the time of hostilities there, he made it a point to go to the hospitals and talk and pray with those who had been wounded. One day as he was visiting a hospital, he met a boy who was lying face downward in a canvas cradle because his spine had been shattered by a bullet. A hole had been cut in the bottom of the cradle so the soldier could see through to the floor.

While Graham was talking to him, the young soldier said, "I would like to see your face, Mr. Graham." Billy Graham got down on his back under the cradle so the boy could look down at Graham's face.

In applying this illustration, J. Ralph Grant said:

> In a rough way that does help us to grasp the fact that God has shown His face in the face of His son, our Lord Jesus Christ, and in order that we might not miss it He stooped to the agony and bloody sweat of the cross. Have you seen the glory of God in the face and hands of Jesus Christ?[5]

> If Jesus Christ is a man,
> And only a man,
> I say that of all mankind,
> I will cleave to Him,
> And to Him will I cleave alway.
> But if Jesus Christ is God,
> And the only God,
> I swear I will follow Him
> Through Heaven and Hell
> The earth, the sea, and the air.[6]

Jesus is "Alpha and Omega," He said. Alpha is "A" in the Greek alphabet and Omega is "Z." Jesus, then, is everything we need from A to Z. He is "the divine alphabet."

He is: Advocate—1 John 2:1; Beloved—Matt. 3:17; Christ—John

1:41; Deliverer—Rom. 11:26; and Eternal life—1 John 5:20.

Also, He is the Friend of sinners—Matt. 11:19; God—John 1:1; I am—John 8:58; and Immortal—1 Tim. 1:17.

He is Jesus—Matt. 1:21; King of Kings—Rev. 17:14; Life—John 14:6; Man of Sorrows—Isa. 53:3; and Nazarene—Matt. 2:23.

Also, He is the Offspring of David—Rev. 22:16; the Only Begotten—John 1:14; the Pearl of Great Price—Matt. 13:46; the Prince of Peace—Isa. 9:6; and Quickening Spirit—1 Cor. 15:45.

He is the Redeemer—Isa. 59:20; Savior—Luke 2:11; Truth—John 14:6; Unspeakable Gift—2 Cor. 9:15; Vine—John 15:1 and Word of Life—1 John 1:1.

Christ is the crimson thread that holds all the Scriptures together. In Genesis He is the seed of woman; in Exodus, the Passover Lamb; in Leviticus, the Atoning Sacrifice; in Numbers, the Smitten Rock; and in Deuteronomy, the Prophet.

In Joshua He is the Captain of the Lord's Host; in Judges, the Deliverer; in Ruth, the Heavenly Kinsman; in the six books of Kings, the promised King; and in Nehemiah, the Restorer of the Nation.

In Esther He is the Advocate; in Job, the Redeemer; in Psalms, All in All; in Proverbs, the Pattern; in Ecclesiastes, God; in the Song of Solomon, the Satisfier.

In the Prophets He is the Coming Prince of Peace; in the Gospels, He is the Christ coming to seek and to save the lost; in the Acts, He is Christ risen; in the Epistles, He is Christ at the Father's right hand; and in the Revelation, He is Christ returning and reigning.

1. Benjamin P. Browne, *Illustrations for Preaching* (Nashville: Broadman Press, 1977), 54.

2. James C. Hefley, *A Dictionary of Illustrations* (Grand Rapids, Mich.: Zondervan Publishing, 1971), 48.

3. Ibid., 49.

4. J. Ralph Grant, *The Word of the Lord for Special Days* (Grand Rapids, Mich.: Baker Book House, 1964), 155-156.

5. From one of J. Ralph Grant's unpublished sermons titled "Christ Makes God Known to Us," 5.

6. Author unknown.

Joy

...Ye rejoice with joy unspeakable and full of glory (1 Pet. 1:8).

In one of his Keswick Week messages, Dr. Paul Rees told about a man from Louisville, Kentucky, who had to travel to St. Louis on business. Since the Christian man had scruples against riding the trains on Sunday, after he finished up his business late Saturday night he had to stay over in St. Louis until the following Monday morning.

On Saturday morning, he left the hotel looking for a place to worship. The streets were quite deserted, but finally he saw a policeman and asked him for directions to the nearest Protestant church.

The stranger thanked the policeman for the information and was about to walk off when he turned and asked the policeman: "Why have you recommended that particular church? There must be several churches nearby that you could have recommended."

The policeman smiled and replied: "I'm not a church man myself, but the people who come out of that church are the happiest looking church-people in St. Louis. I thought that would be the kind of church you would like to attend."[1]

J. Ralph Grant tells in one of his messages about an ad that appeared some years ago in the London Times: "Wanted by an invalid lady, a housekeeper; must be a good church woman to take care of the house and four servants; a cheerful Christian, if possible."

The word *joy* appears about 150 times in the Bible. Add *joyous* and *joyful* and the number swells to about 200. And the word *rejoice* appears about the same number of times.[2]

Perhaps synonyms for *joy* would be happiness, gladness, merriment, delight, and pleasure only to mention a few.

Joy should not depend upon circumstances. The late Dr. Millard A. Jenkens, who served First Baptist Church, Abilene, Texas, tells a story about singing evangelist Homer Rodeheaver's encounter with an invalid.

The young man asked Mr. Rodeheaver to sing a special song. Rodeheaver asked, "And what song do you wish sung?"

The young man replied, "I want you to sing that one about the sunshine. I have a lot of your songs that I play on my Victrola. But I have so much sunshine in my life, I want to hear the song about the sunshine."

When Rodeheaver asked the young man how he could talk about having so much sunshine in his life when he was an invalid, the young man replied: "I'm sorry for well folks sometimes because they have so much to do they haven't time to get aquainted with Jesus."[3]

One of John Wesley's preacher friends was John Nelson. Nelson tells about the time he and Wesley were preaching in Cornwall. When they went to bed they didn't have the most comfortable conveniences. In fact, they had to sleep on the floor. Nelson said for his pillow he used Burkitt's *Notes on the New Testament* and Wesley used Nelson's coat.

After preaching in the Cornwall area for three weeks, Nelson reports, Wesley turned over one morning about 3:00 AM and seeing that Nelson was awake, Wesley slapped Nelson on the side and said: "Brother Nelson, let us be of good cheer: I have one whole side yet, for the skin is off but on one side!"[4]

Nelson reported that they didn't have very much to eat. One morning Wesley stopped his horse to pick the blackberries along the way and said to Brother Nelson: "Brother Nelson, we ought to be thankful that there are plenty of blackberries; for this is the best country I ever saw for getting a stomach, but the worst I ever saw for getting food!"[5]

William Barclay added, "Christian joy made Wesley able to accept the great blows of life, and to greet the lesser discomforts with a jest. If the Christian walks with Christ, he must of necessity walk with joy."[6]

Benjamin Browne tells an interesting story about an occasion when the American preacher Theodore Cuyler was visiting the great London preacher Charles H. Spurgeon. Carefree and in high spirits they roamed through the woods and across the meadows telling each other funny stories and reminiscing about humorous things that had happened in their respective ministries. Their laughter was full of joy and often deep and prolonged. After they had exhausted themselves in laughter over one particularly amusing story, Spurgeon suggested they kneel down in the meadow and praise God for laughter. Reverently, the two great preachers knelt together and thanked God for the wonderful gift of a light and joyous heart that he given to them.

Joy is a gift of God that only we humans of his creation can enjoy.[7]

1. *The Keswick Week*, (London: Marshall, Morgan & Scott, Ltd., 1958), 133.

2. Robert J. Dean, *God's Big Little Words* (Nashville: Broadman Press, 1975), 85.

3. Millard A. Jenkins, *Special Day Sermons* (Nashville: Broadman Press, 1942), 13.

4. Adapted from William Barclay, *The Letters to the Philippians, Colossians, & Thessalonians (Rev. Ed.)* (Philadelphia: Westminster Press/John Knox Press, 1975), 64. Used by permission.

5. Ibid, 65.

6. Ibid, 65.

7. Benjamin P. Brown, *Illustrations for Preaching* (Nashville: Broadman Press, Nashville, 1977), 119-120.

Judgment

For we must all appear before the judgment seat of Christ (2 Cor. 5:10).

That we must all stand before God on the day of judgment is a scriptural truth that cannot be denied. Jesus clearly warns us about it.

In *Shields of Brass*, Roy Angell wrote that once the editor of a newspaper sent well-known writer Bruce Barton to the hospital to talk to Russell Conwell. Conwell, a Baptist clergyman, founder of Philadelphia's Temple University, and author of the world-famous classic *Acres of Diamonds*, was critically ill.

Barton told Conwell that all the world knew about his great work and his famous lecture, "Acres of Diamonds," which he had delivered hundreds of times. But, Barton said, he had been sent to find out if Conwell had any fear as he came to the close of his life.

Conwell hesitated a few minutes and then told Barton that as a boy of fourteen on a New England farm he learned an unforgettable lesson.

Conwell continued. "One day my dad called me into the house and told me that he had to go into town to take care of some business and that he would be gone a day or so. He said the bottom land needed to be plowed, and that some of the cattle had broken through the fence and they needed to be brought back and the fence needed to be fixed. He said the wagon needed to be greased so they could use it upon his return to haul corn to market."

Then Conwell said that as his father left he said to his son, "Do the best you can."

"The next night I dragged into the house bone tired just as my dad returned from town. The first thing he wanted to know was how I had made out in his absence," Conwell said.

"I got them all done," Conwell said with pride.

"You got them all done?" his father asked. "Did you get the bottom land plowed? Are the cows back in the field and is the fence fixed? Did you get the wagon greased? That's a whole lot of work, Son. Do you mean you got it all done?" the elder Conwell asked.

"Beaming with pride, I said, 'Yes, Father, I got them all done.' "

Then Russell Conwell said his dad looked straight at him and said, "A good day's work, Russ."

Conwell continued. "Bruce," he said, "Before long my Heavenly Father and I are going to meet face to face. I think He will put his arm around me and say to me, 'Son, you've done a good day's work; a good day's work.' "

Barton said he tiptoed out of the room feeling that he had stood on holy ground.[1]

It is reported that the thing that made William Booth, the founder of the Salvation Army, such a passionate preacher was the statement of the man who claimed to be an infidel: "If I believed what you Christians say you believe with reference to the coming judgment and day of reckoning, with the resultant eternal lostness of the impenitent Christ-rejecters, then I would crawl on my bare knees on crushed glass all over London, England, night and day telling men and women to flee from the wrath to come!"[2]

It is told that Philip of Macedon, the father of Alexander the Great, fell asleep one day while hearing a case. Waking suddenly and not having all the facts of the case straight, Philip passed an unjust sentence on the man who was at Phillip's mercy.

Stung by the sentence, the poor man cried out, "I appeal!"

Startled, the king asked, "And to whom do you appeal?"

The man replied, "From the king who was sleeping to the king who is waking."

The king was so moved by the man's logical appeal that he reversed the judgment he had passed.[3]

But when we stand before Him who is the just Judge and who never sleeps, there will be no chance for appeal.

In his book, *Letters to the Seven Churches and Other Sermons*, J. Ralph Grant tells about a sheriff who was not a Christian. He was a courageous, good, moral man, but he was lost. The pastor in the community where the sheriff lived was concerned about his friend's salvation. One day the pastor spoke to the sheriff about trusting in Christ as his personal Savior and the sheriff was agitated. He replied that he would not be scared into "religion" because he was not afraid to die.

But the pastor gently reminded the sheriff that death is not all and that beyond the grave there is judgment and eternity.

The pastor's words penetrated the heart of the sheriff like an arrow and he replied that although he was not afraid to die, he trembled when he thought of the judgment to come.[4]

1. Roy Angell, *Shields of Brass* (Nashville: Broadman Press, 1965), 109-110.

2. Walter B. Knight, *Knight's Master Book of New Illustrations* (Grand Rapids, Mich.: Wm. B. Eerdmans Publishing Co., 1956), 351. Used by permission.

3. Elon Foster, *6,000 Classic Sermon Illustrations* (Grand Rapids, Mich.: Baker Book House, 1974), n.p.n.

4. J. Ralph Grant, *Letters To The Seven Churches and Other Sermons* (Grand Rapids, Mich.: Baker Book House, 1962), 84.

Kind/Kindness

Be ye kind one to another (Eph. 4:32).

Albrecht (Albert) Durer (1471-1528) was one of the leading German artists of the Renaissance.

The son of a poor Hungarian goldsmith, Durer wanted to be an artist even from his boyhood, but money was scarce. He finally got an opportunity to study with an outstanding teacher, but it was understood that young Albert would have to pay his way.

According to R. L. Middleton, Durer found a friend who also wanted to study with the master teacher, and the two decided to share an apartment in order to cut their expenses. But times were very hard and the two barely got by. Durer's friend, an older man, said he would go to work for a while to support them while Albert studied. Then after Albert had begun to sell some of his art, the older man said he would go back to study under the teacher.

The older man got a job in a restaurant scrubbing floors, washing dishes and doing any menial job available to earn money. The hours were long and hard and the weeks dragged into months. But Durer's friend worked willingly because he knew it was worth it.

Albert finally sold one of his wood carvings and joyously bounded into the room with enough money to pay the rent and buy food for several months. As he rushed into the room he was thinking to himself, *Now, my Friend, you can have your chance.*

The two friends rejoiced together over Albert's good fortune and the older man returned to his art studies, brushes, and canvases.

But it was too late. The long hard hours and the menial work had taken their toll. His fingers were stiff and he couldn't hold the brush correctly and give the canvas the necessary gentle strokes. Though he tried again and again, it was to no avail and sadly he knew he would have to give up his lifelong dream of becoming an artist.

Durer was heartbroken when he realized what had happened to his friend and the price he had paid to encourage the young, struggling artist. Although he knew he couldn't give back to his friend the supple fingers and gentle touch needed, he could and would take care of him.

One day Durer entered their room unexpectedly and found his friend, with hands folded, kneeling in prayer. Catching a glimpse of the calloused hands and large protruding veins in his friend's hands, Durer had the inspiration he needed.

So, in honor of his friend, Durer set about to paint what turned out to be one of his greatest masterpieces. And millions have been blessed by his beautiful, masterful picture titled, *Praying Hands.* [1]

Late one night many years ago, an elderly couple walked into a small, third-rate hotel in Philadelphia to rent a room for the night. There was a big convention going on in town and though the couple had checked with several hotels, they had been unable to find a room.

The young clerk on duty told the couple that he couldn't help them because the hotel, like others, was filled to capacity. As they turned to walk away, the young man was touched by their weariness and called to them: "I have an idea. You won't be able to find a room in town tonight so there is no need to look any further. I have a room in the hotel and I won't get off work until morning. It isn't much, but the sheets are clean and you can at least get a good night's sleep."

The elderly couple protested that they didn't want to inconvenience the young clerk, but the clerk gave them the key and insisted that they sleep in his bed. (Another version of the story says that the clerk slept on a couch in the lobby.)

The next morning when the elderly couple came down to check out, rested and refreshed from a good night's sleep, they thanked the young clerk profusely. "You are too fine a clerk to spend the rest of your life working in this kind of hotel," the elderly man said. "Someday I will build a hotel for you and let you run it."

The clerk took the elderly man's compliment with a grain of salt, thinking to himself, *Yes, I bet you will build me a hotel!*

Two years later he received a letter from the man. Although the clerk had almost forgotten about the incident, the older man was writing to invite the clerk to come to New York City to visit them. Included in the letter was a round-trip train ticket to New York.

When the young man was met by the couple in New York City, they took him to the corner of Fifth Avenue and Thirty-fourth Street and pointed to a newly constructed, magnificent building standing on that thoroughfare. It looked more like a castle than just a building—superior in design and construction from the foundation to the roof.

"This is the hotel I promised you," the elderly man said. "It's yours to manage as long as you want it."

"But you must be joking," the young man replied.

"No, it isn't a joke," the older man said. "I told you I would build you a hotel to run, and there it is."

The man's name was William Waldorf Astor. The young clerk was George C. Boldt. And the hotel was the original Waldorf-Astoria Hotel, one of the most magnificent hotels ever constructed.

The young man learned that kindness pays off.[2]

After Confederate General Robert E. Lee retired from military life, he was named president of Washington and Lee University in Lexington, Virginia. Originally named Washington Academy because of a $50,000 gift from George Washington, the name of the school was changed in 1871 in honor of Lee who served as its president from 1865-1870.

While Lee was president of the University, a new student came into Lee's office and asked for a copy of the school's rules and regulations.

Lee replied that the school had no printed rules. Our only rule is kindness, Lee replied.

Confederate President Jefferson Davis, it is said, once asked General Robert E. Lee for his opinion of General Whiting. Lee told David that Whiting was an exceptionally qualified man. A friend who was listening protested to Lee: "Don't you know what mean things General Whiting has been saying about you?" the friend asked.

"Yes, I know what he has been saying about me," General Lee replied. "But President Davis did not ask me what General Whiting thinks of me. He asked me what I think of General Whiting."

1. R. L. Middleton, *The Gift of Love* (Nashville: Broadman Press, 1976), 73-74.

2. Charles L. Allen, *Roads to Radiant Living* (Old Tappan, N. J.: Fleming H. Revell Co., 1951), 107; Fowler's personal File "Kindness"—an article by Joe L. Ingram.

Laugh/Laughter

Blessed are ye that weep now: for ye shall laugh (Luke 6:21).

The Bible says that, "a merry heart doeth good like a medicine" (Prov. 17:22).

Living in a world that seems to be insane most of the time, we need to find every opportunity to laugh.

Texas minister and educator William E. Thorn says: "Stop taking yourself so seriously. Some cannot see the humor in any situation. Humor is a good means of relieving tension, dispelling fear, and cooling anger. Try to develop humor as a personal trait. It will keep from an overestimation of your own importance."

Thorn says that "Wit is the salt of the conversation, not the food." He quotes the Psalmist, "Then was our mouth filled with laughter, and our tongue was singing; then said they among the heathen, the Lord hath done great things for them" (Ps. 126:2).

Dr. J. D. Grey was my friend. When I was pastor in Mississippi, he was pastor in New Orleans and I had the opportunity frequently to profit from his friendship. Grey was always good for a laugh.

In his book *Epitaphs for Eager Preachers*, Grey shows us that one can get a laugh almost anywhere.

Grey says that a preacher was conducting a funeral service of a certain disreputable citizen. Waxing eloquent in eulogizing the brother, the preacher said some things hard for the widow, who had lived with the deceased for years, to accept.

Finally, when she could take it no longer, she said to her son, "Boy, just go up there and look and see if that's your Pappy in the coffin!"

Grey relates that at the funeral service of a prominent politician, a lawyer came in late and sat down on the back pew by the side of another lawyer friend.

"How long has the parson been preaching?" the lawyer, who had arrived late, asked his friend.

"Oh, I think about forty years," the friend replied.

"Well then I think I'll stay," the lawyer replied, "for he must be about through."

And his friend replied dryly, "Oh, he just opened for the defense."

About laughter, Germany's famous writer Johann Goethe, said: "Men show their characters in nothing more clearly than in what they think laughable."

Thomas Carlyle, English writer and historian, said about laughter: "How much lies in laughter: the cipher-key, wherewith we decipher the whole man."

Another English writer, Charles Lamb, said about laughter: "A laugh is worth a hundred groans in any market."

Novelist William Thackery said: "A good laugh is sunshine in the house."

Lost

For the Son of man is come to seek and to save that which was lost (Luke 19:10).

To be lost means to be separated from God. It is to be estranged from Him. Jesus uses it nine times in the New Testament to describe those who are unsaved. It is used in Luke 15, in the parable of lost things, more times than any other place in the New Testament.

Clarence Darrow (1857-1938), who opposed William Jennings Bryan in the famous Scopes Trial in 1925, claimed to be an agnostic. In his seventy-seventh year and near the end of his life, Darrow said: "All my life I have been seeking definite proof of God—something I could put my finger on, and say, 'This is a fact.' But my doubts are at rest now. I know that such fact does not exist. When I die, as I shall soon, my body will decay, my mind will decay, and my intellect will be gone. My soul? There is no such thing."[1]

Rodney Smith, better known as evangelist "Gipsy" Smith, was born in England in 1860 and died in 1947.

Smith told that when his father was a young man, a band of fifty or more gypsies was working on a farm near Tunbridge, England. They were moving from one field to another by wagon when they came to an old wooden bridge over which they thought they could pass safely. The river was high because of the heavy rain and as the wagons pulled down into the water-covered roadway close to the bridge, the women became frightened, startling the horses. Before the horses could be stopped, the wagon crashed into the sides of the rotten structure and all the riders were thrown into the swift current.

Smith said that, according to his father, a brave young gypsy grabbed hold of one of the horses as it drifted by. The boy was looking for his mother. When he spotted her struggling helplessly in the water, he reached out to her but she struggled so that he could not hold on to her. Soon she had sunk beneath the deadly waters.

On the day of the funeral, the survivors gathered to bury their thirty-nine relatives who had perished in the water. But the young man was so overcome with grief that he forgot the crowd and the service that was in progress and fell down beside his mother and wept: "Mother, Mother, I tried to save you. I did all a man could do to save you, but you would not let me."[2]

Mark Twain was the pen name of Samuel Langhorne Clemens (1835-1910). He is best known for his novels *The Adventures of Tom Sawyer* and *The Adventures of Huckleberry Finn*.

Benjamin P. Browne relates that once when Twain and his daughter, Susy, were in Europe, he received an invitation from the German emperor to dine at the palace. Susy, proud of her daddy, exclaimed: "Daddy, you know most everybody in the whole world, don't you, except God?"[3]

Aaron Burr (1756-1836) was vice president of the United States from 1801-1805 under President Thomas Jefferson. Both Burr's father and grandfather had been president of Princeton College—now Princeton University. Burr was graduated from Princeton in 1772. His grandfather was the renowned colonial preacher Jonathan Edwards.

When a spiritual revival swept Princeton, Burr's response was, "I follow only reason." But as the revival continued, Burr sought advice from Dr. John Whitherspoon, president of the college. However, Whitherspoon discouraged Burr from getting too caught up in the emotion of the revival.

One version of the account details that Burr went back to his dormitory room, threw open the window, and shouted out across the campus, "Goodbye, God!"

Burr considered at one time becoming a minister. But, apparently, as he continued to reject the claims of Christ his feelings changed. Referring to his grandfather, Jonathan Edwards, who was one of the chief personalities of the Great Awakening in New England, Burr stated: "I hold nothing but contempt for the teachings of my grandfather. I prefer a soldier's life."

Burr is best remembered for the great failure he made of his life. He was defeated for the presidency of the United States both in 1796 and 1800. In 1800, he and Jefferson tied and the House of Representatives had to take thirty-six ballots to break the tie. The influence of Alexander Hamilton defeated Burr.

Burr ran for governor of New York in 1804. Again, Hamilton was the reason for his defeat. Challenging Hamilton to a duel on July 11, 1804, the men faced each other at Weehawken, New Jersey, and Burr fatally wounded Hamilton. Both New Jersey and New York grand juries indicted Burr for murder, but he fled South before he could be arrested. Returning to Washington when Congress reconvened, Vice President Burr presided over the term until it ended.

A politically ruined man, Burr was arrested in New Orleans for treason, accused of mustering an army to invade Mexico. Tried for treason in 1807, he was acquitted but his reputation was ruined. For a while he lived in Europe, but he returned to the United States in 1812 under an assumed name. Taking up the practice of law in New York City, Burr prospered. On his deathbed in 1836, again Burr was pressed to trust in Christ as his Savior. His reply was, "On that subject I am coy."[4]

Burr's philosophy, apparently, was the same as that of William Ernest Henley who wrote:

> Out of the night that covers me,
> Black as the Pit from pole to pole,
> I thank whatever gods may be
> For my unconquerable soul.

1. Millard Alford Jenkins, *Special Day Sermons* (Nashville: Broadman Press, 1942), 59.

2. Clyde E. Fant, Jr., William M. Pinson, Jr., *20 Centuries of Great Preaching, Vol. VII* (Waco, Tex.: Word Books, Inc., 1971).

3. Benjamin P. Browne, *Illustrations for Preaching* (Nashville: Broadman Press, 1977), 49.

4. James C. Hefley, *A Dictionary of Illustrations* (Grand Rapids, Mich.: Zondervan Publishing House, 1971), 93-94.

Love

Greater love hath no man than this, that a man lay down his life for his friends (John 15:13).

Regardless of how disreputably one may have lived, there is always something left to love. In the movie and book *A Raisin In The Sun*, the family prodigal, Walter, has gambled away his sister's college fund. She has given up on him, but their mother pleads with her to be patient with him and to love him. Resentfully, the sister screams out that there is nothing left to love, but the wise mother replies: "There's always something left to love. And if you ain't learned that, you ain't learned nothing."[1]

It is the nature of love to sacrifice for others. Sir Wilfred Grenfell, noted British missionary and physician to Labrador, saw a patient one day whose hands had been blown off. Bone-grafting two "flippers" on the stubs that remained, Grenfell then took strips of flesh from his own body to cover the "flippers" that served as the man's hands. Grenfell thought what he had done was not spectacular, but those who saw what he had done called it impossible.[2]

Robert Louis Stevenson, the noted Scottish writer, fell in love with American Fanny Osbourne after she had left her husband to live abroad. When Stevenson told his father, who lived in Edinburgh, Scotland, about his love for married Fanny, the rift between Louis and his father widened.

Stevenson crossed the ocean and America low on funds and poor in health out of love for Fanny. He arrived in California gallant but physically weak and announced to his Fanny that his father had cut off all funds and that Stevenson was on his own.

Fanny sought a divorce while Robert lived on seventy cents a day in San Francisco. He sold his last resources, his books which were in Scotland, to subsist. Word of Robert's penury reached his father, Thomas, "that stormy and tender old man," as Robert called him, and he cabled Louis the encouraging message: "Count on me for 250 pounds a year!"

Robert and Fanny were married at the home of a Presbyterian minister in San Francisco. Their love was strong and special until Stevenson died at forty-four on the island of Samoa.

The love story of Robert Browning and Elizabeth Barrett is well-known to lovers of literature. The love story of these two great English poets is one of the sweetest stories on record.

She was born in 1806, but her health began to decline in 1835 after the Barrett family moved to London. Soon she became a permanent invalid and it seemed she was doomed to spend the remainder of her days confined to her house.

In 1845, after some of her poems were published, she and Robert Browning began to correspond. In 1846 they were married. During their courtship, Elizabeth had written *Sonnets from the Portuguese*, in which she recorded the growth of her great love for Browning. These sonnets are probably the best known love poems in the English language.

It was Browning who suggested the title for the sonnets. Elizabeth had a dark complexion, as someone from Portugal might have. Robert had teasingly called Elizabeth "my little Portuguese" so *Sonnets from the Portuguese* seemed an appropriate title.

The two were so happy and so much in love. The couple moved to Italy where the warm climate and Browning's strong love for Elizabeth helped to restore her health. She died in Florence in 1861, where she is buried. Browning lived until 1889.

"To what do you owe your success?" she was once asked.

"I had a friend," she replied.

That friend was her lover, husband, mentor, and companion—Robert Browning.

Charles and Mary Lamb were brother and sister. Both were English writers. Mary was born in 1764 and Charles in 1775. Charles's love for Mary and his devotion to her were very strong.

At times Mary suffered bouts of temporary insanity. In 1796, while Charles and Mary were both still living at home, their lives were darkened by a tragedy of unspeakably great proportions. In a moment of insanity, Mary picked up a kitchen knife and stabbed their mother to death. The court understood Mary's mental problems and put her in the custody of Charles, and she lived with him most of the time until he died in 1834.

The great Baptist preacher, the late Dr. George W. Truett of Dallas, writes about Lamb's love for Mary: "I think there is nothing in history more touching than the behavior of Charles Lamb, the brilliant British essayist and critic, who devoted his best hours to his sister, Mary, who had recurring spells of insanity. Charles Lamb could soothe her into sanity as nobody else in the world could. She adored her brother. He was to be seen many times in the morning, e'er the sun came up, traversing the lanes of England, talking with Mary, telling her about the singing birds, and the smiling flowers, seeking to keep back that encroaching wave of insanity as it persisted in coming again and again. Glorious!"[3]

Glorious, indeed, was his love for poor Mary.

Truett, who served First Baptist Church, Dallas, Texas, as pastor for forty-seven years, wrote in his book *Follow Thou Me*:

> The story is told that in one of our well-known art galleries, an old man was one day seen gazing earnestly at a picture of the thorn-crowned Christ. Involuntarily, the expression broke from his lips: "Bless him! I love him!" A stranger standing near, heard the old man's words, and clasped his hand and said: "Brother, I love him, too." And then a third, and a fourth, and still others, who before had been strangers to one another were brought together by their common love for the crucified Lord.[4]

The late R. L. Middleton wrote about a convict who was in the state prison for women at Sherborn, Massachusetts. Mrs. Ellen C. Johnson, the warden, related that once there was a woman in the prison who was all but incorrigible. She resisted every influence to make her conform to the rules of the prison.

Mrs. Johnson ordered a painting of Jesus to be placed in the chapel thinking the picture of Jesus would have a good effect on the woman. It was a life-size picture of Jesus forgiving the sinful woman in John's gospel, and the picture was well-lighted so that it was dramatic and moving to behold.

On the evening the painting was to be unveiled, Mrs. Johnson seated the difficult prisoner on the front pew, directly in front of the picture of the Savior. The prisoners were not warned ahead of time what they would see when they went to the chapel. So, when the lights were brought down low the story of Jesus forgiving the woman was told from the gospel. The lights were then turned on the picture, the veil was taken away, and there was the striking picture of the brokenhearted, sinful woman kneeling at the feet of the Savior. Jesus was saying to her, "Neither do I condemn thee: Go, and sin no more."

A subdued applause burst from the inmates followed by stillness. Suddenly, the face of the hardened woman flushed and lighted up as though an old, forgotten ember had been fanned to a flame in her heart. She began to weep and when the convicts were instructed to stand and return to their cells, she sat riveted to her chair staring in adoring love at the face of her new Savior and Lord. Where everything else had failed to change the woman's life, the love of Jesus had succeeded.[5]

Scottish novelist Robert Louis Stevenson (1850-1894) probably is best known for his novel *Treasure Island.*

Stevenson's health was never very good. In 1888 he went with his family to Samoa in the South Pacific and lived there until he died. Upon his death, sixty Samoans carried his body to the top of Mount Vaea where he lies buried today.

Stevenson involved himself in the lives of the Samoan people. He took an interest in them and the community. One of his good friends, Mataafa, was the native ruler. When Mataafa and several of the tribal chiefs were imprisoned, apparently because of some political problems, Stevenson did not forget them. Frequently he visited them in prison, bringing gifts and encouragement.

When Mataafa and the chiefs were freed, they felt such gratitude for what Stevenson had done for them that they determined to find some way to express their appreciation. When it was suggested that they could cut a road through the dense brush to Stevenson's house, they immediately went to work to build the road.

Finally, after much labor and sacrifice, the road to Stevenson's house was completed. And the natives called it "The Road of The Loving Heart."[6]

1. James E. Hightower Jr., *Illustrating Paul's Letter To The Romans* (Nashville: Broadman Press, 1984), 59.

2. Donald Culross Peattie, *Lives Of Destiny* (New York: New American Library, 1954), 175.

3. George W. Truett, *Sermons From Paul* (Nashville: Broadman Press, 1947), 133.

4. George W. Truett, *Follow Thou Me* (Nashville: Sunday School Board of the Southern Baptist Convention, 1932), 66.

5. R. L. Middleton, *Don't Disappoint God* (Nashville: Broadman Press, 1951), 160-161.

6. William L. Stidger, *There Are Sermons In Stories* (New York and Nashville: Abington-Cokesbury Press, 1942), 69-70.

Man / Woman

Man shall not live by bread alone (Matt. 4:4).

In his book *The Origin of All Things*, Herschel H. Hobbs says that Archbishop James Ussher (1581-1656) computed that creation occurred in 4004 B.C. Cambridge Professor Lightfoot (1602-1675) declared that the world was created between Oct. 18-24, 4004 B.C. He went on to state that man was created at 9:00 AM on Oct. 23, 4004 B.C.! Hobbs says he wished Lightfoot had computed it just one day later so that it would have fallen on Hobbs's birthday![1]

When mankind was created, no one but God can say. But that mankind is a divine miracle of creation no one can truthfully deny.

According to cardiologists, the average human heart may pump as much as 36.8 million times a year. If you live to be seventy, your heart will beat no less than 2.5 billion times.

Although the figures vary, according to those who are supposed to know, the human brain contains between 30 and 50 billion cells. It has been estimated that the number of possible circuits in the brain is greater than the number of atoms in the universe. It is a little organ, weighing only thirty-five ounces, but its capacity exceeds that of the most-complex computer ever designed.

One writer has suggested that if the cells of the brain were only worth a nickel each, and if each connection those cells makes is worth only one penny, the value of the human brain would exceed one quintillion dollars. That's one billion dollars times one billion dollars or a one with eighteen zeros after it. We must agree with the psalmist: "I will praise thee; for I am fearfully and wonderfully made: marvelous are thy works;

and that my soul knoweth right well" (Psalms 139:14).

A black baby was born to a slave mother near Diamond Grove, Missouri, about the time the Civil War ended. One night, the infant and his mother were stolen by night riders and taken to Arkansas. The owner hired John Bentley to bring the baby and his mother back to Missouri, but when Bentley returned several days later he brought back only the baby and he was nearly dead.

When the master asked Bentley where the baby had been found, Bentley replied: " 'Oh, him, they just give him to some women folk down by Conway. He ain't worth nothin.' "[2]

But George Washington Carver, the little black infant, grew up to become one of the greatest scientists the South ever produced. The South was economically depressed because the boll weevil was destroying the cotton crop year after year, and Carver encouraged the farmers to diversify and to plant peanuts, sweet potatoes, and so forth. From the peanut, Carver developed more than 300 products—instant coffee, soap, ink. And from the sweet potato he developed more than 118 products including shoe polish, candy, and flour. From the pecan Carver developed more than 75 products.

His humble yet brilliant life was a magnificent contradiction of Bentley's analysis of the half-dead infant he brought back to Missouri from Arkansas: "He ain't worth nothin'."

At a dinner honoring the late black gospel singer Ethel Waters, evangelist Billy Graham asked Waters how she had been able to retain such a positive attitude in spite of racial discrimination. Waters replied: "I have lived out of the belief that God creates no inferior products. When it comes to human beings there are no factory seconds, castoffs, or rejects."[3]

Waters said, "God don't make no junk."

In the heart of London stands the magnificent St. Paul's Cathedral. During the second World War, St. Paul's was bombed by the Nazis. One day in papers all across America there appeared a picture of the bombed-out ruins of St. Paul's. Above the picture was the caption: "Designed By

Sir Christopher Wren—Destroyed by Hitler."

The same thing can be said about mankind. Men and women were designed and created by God Almighty. We have been destroyed by sin and only Jesus can recreate us.

After General Ulysses S. Grant had been made head of the Union forces in the Civil War, it is said that hope was revived in the North and among the Union forces in the field. However, a Union company officer observed that only time would tell whether the General's first name was really "Ulysses" or "Useless."[4]

But Jesus, who died for each of us, says that no one is useless!

The late, well-known Anglican preacher William Barclay wrote in his commentary on Luke about a wandering, elderly scholar of the middle ages named Muretus.

Muretus became ill and was confined to a hospital for those who were too poor to pay. As the doctors stood over the old saint discussing his case in Latin, they had no idea that the old scholar could understand every word they spoke.

"He's nothing but a worthless wanderer," they concluded. "And he isn't worth saving but we could use him for experiments," they agreed. Having heard all he cared to hear, the old saint surprised them as he answered in Latin, "Call no man worthless for whom Christ died."[5]

Henry Alford Porter wrote:

> The Greeks had a beautiful word for man—'anthropos,' meaning the being with the upturned face. Men are queer things. Man is so made that he cannot be content with forever looking down. He may look down a long time, so long that he almost forgets there's anything else, anything above, forgets that he was made for God—until something happens, some crisis comes. And then he remembers and looks up.[6]

1. Herschel H. Hobbs, *The Origin of All Things* (Waco, Tex.: Word Books, 1975, 11.

2. Lawrence Elliott, *George Washington Carver: The Man Who Overcame* (Englewood Cliffs, N. J.: Prentice-Hall Inc., 1966), 14.

3. *Proclaim* Magazine, July 1980, 35.

4. Bruce Catton, *A Stillness At Appomattox* (Garden City, N. Y.: Doubleday & Co. Inc., 1953), 44.

5. James E. Hightower, Jr., compiler, *Illustrating Paul's Letter to the Romans* (Nashville: Broadman Press, 1984), 38.

6. Henry Alford Porter, *Toward the Sun Rising* (Nashville: Broadman Press, 1947), 49.

Mercy

Blessed are the merciful: for they shall obtain mercy (Matt. 5:7).

Baptist theologian E. Y. Mullins wrote that "mercy is love expressing itself in forgiveness and remission of penalty from the guilty." It is God's love reaching out toward the guilty, he declared.

English preacher Richard Baxter wisely said: "Oh Lord, it must be great mercy or no mercy, for little mercy is of no use to me."

Nicolaus Copernicus was a Polish astronomer and scientist. He was born at Thorn (or Torun), Poland, in 1473, and died in 1543. He founded modern-day astronomy with his theory that the earth moves around the sun.

Until Copernicus's time, astronomers accepted Ptolemy's theory formulated 1400 years earlier that the sun moves around the earth. Ptolemy thought that the earth was the center of the universe and did not move. But Copernicus proved him wrong. A devout Catholic, Copernicus received both master's and doctor's degrees and, in addition, studied medicine.

Copernicus's picture hangs in St. John's Church in Thorn, Poland, his hometown. Beneath the picture is his epitaph and confession of faith. It is a strong testimony to the mercy of God.

> I do not ask the grace which Thou didst give Saint Paul;
> nor can I dare to ask the grace which Thou didst grant to
> Saint Peter;
> but, the mercy which Thou didst show to the Dying Robber,
> that mercy show to me.

Robert J. Dean tells about a sign that illustrates the contradiction between what we profess and what we practice. On the property of a certain religious order, this sign appeared:

KEEP OUT

SISTERS OF MERCY.[1]

There is an ancient legend about the two thieves who were crucified with Jesus. According to the mythical story, the names of the two thieves were Titus and Dumacus. When they were crucified, they were old.

Many years before that sad Good Friday when Jesus and the two thieves were crucified, Joseph and Mary were fleeing to Egypt with the baby Jesus. As they fled, their caravan was assaulted by these two thieves. Dumacus wanted to kill Joseph and Mary and the baby Jesus, but Titus persuaded his bloodthirsty companion to spare their lives.

Then, according to the legend, Titus said to the Christ child: "O blessed Child, if the day should ever come when I shall need mercy, then on that day remember this deed."[2]

Elon Foster recalled that during one of the Battles of Bull Run in the Civil War, a wounded soldier fell on his knees and cried out, "God have mercy on my soul."

The cry became contagious. One soldier after another took it up until a loud chorus could be heard through the whole army in that section.

This is the prayer the publican cried out to God and by which he was saved, and it is the cry that every lost sinner must cry to God if he is to have forgiveness and life everlasting.[3]

Richard Baxter, the early-day English preacher, emphasized that mercy is personal when he said: "I conceive there could be no word so strong as the 'whosoever' in the gospel offer. If God had put my name in his word, and made it an express revelation that Richard Baxter might be saved, it would not have been half so strong, because there might have been many Richard Baxters, and how could I be certified that it was for me especially the word was meant? But when he has said 'whosoever will,' then I can have no doubt. The word is so inclusive, that none need fear exclusion; so gracious that none need apprehend rejection."[4]

1. Robert J. Dean, *God's Big Little Words* (Nashville: Broadman Press, 1975), 43.

2. Clarence E. Macartney, *Macartney's Illustrations* (New York and Nashville: Abingdon-Cokesbury Press, 1945), 390.

3. Elon Foster, *6,000 Classic Sermon Illustrations* (Grand Rapids, Mich.: Baker Book House, 1974), 568.

4. Ibid., 568.

Miracles

Jesus of Nazareth, a man approved of God among you by miracles and wonders and signs (Acts 2:22).

Why should one doubt the miracle of the great fish swallowing Jonah? Jesus didn't (see Matt. 12:38-40).

An author unknown to me has written a startling testimony that should dispel any doubts about the miracle of Jonah's survival. The author relates the harrowing experience of James Bartley who was swallowed by "a great fish" and lived to tell about it.

Of significance is an article that appeared in *The Literary Digest* shortly before the turn of the present century, giving a circumstantial account of the case of James Bartley, a seaman on the whaler *Star of the East*.

In February 1891, this ship launched two boats to capture a huge whale sighted at some distance. It was harpooned and given its death wound. While writhing in agony, it demolished one of the boats with its tail, but all the sailors except two were rescued. The body of one man was recovered; James Bartley, however, could not be found. It took the crew a day and a night to cut up the captured whale. When the creature's stomach was opened, James Bartley was found unconscious but living. After three weeks he was well enough to give an account of what happened. He recalled being swallowed and being forced down the slippery throat by the muscular contractions. The heat, he said, was so terrific as to make him lose consciousness. Following treatment in a London hospital, he recovered completely, but his skin was permanently tanned by the action of the gastric juices.[1]

Miracles abound all around us, but we are so used to them that we are blind to them. Consider, for example, the miracle of the human heart.

The heart is an organ that weighs about twelve ounces, but if the heart beats at seventy-two beats per minute, it pumps through itself forty-five pounds of blood per minute, 2700 pounds per hour, and 32.4 tons per day. It is a muscle that never rests except between beats. Every thirty seconds all the blood in the body passes through the heart. It has a grip greater than that of one's fist. The two ventricles of the heart hold an average of ten ounces of blood which is pumped out at each beat.

What a miracle is this little organ. It does about one-fifth of the mechanical work of the body and exerts enough energy each hour to lift its own weight 13,000 feet into the air.[2]

To send the blood as far away as one's two feet, the heart must overcome a resistance of 12,600 pounds.

What more can be said about this miracle? The heart's wall has three layers. The innermost layer lines its four chambers. The right side of the heart receives deoxygenated blood from the tissues and pumps it to the lungs. But the left side receives oxygenated blood from the lungs and pumps it to the tissues.

The heart, which we don't hear beat as we go about our daily routine, emits two sounds: the first, prolonged dull sound comes from the contraction of the heart's two lower chambers, tension of the valves, and impact against the chest wall. The second sound, shorter and higher-pitched, results when the aortic and pulmonary valves close.[3]

Consider the miracle of light. What is it? The truth is, we don't know. Light travels from the sun to the earth—93 million miles—in seven minutes. And the piece of coal that drives the furnaces of industry is nothing but stored sunlight that shone down upon the earth ages ago. In that piece of coal are all the colors of the spectrum of the sun. From coal which is stored sunlight, can be extracted all the perfumes known to man—the fragrance from flowers that grew long ago. And also from this organic miracle of God can be made both dynamite and many of the healing medicines that mend bodies today.[4]

1. Author unknown, (from J. B. Fowler's personal file).
2. Augustus H. Strong, *Systematic Theology, Vol. II* (Philadelphia: Judson Press, 1956),

411.

3. "Triangle—"Southern Baptist Hospital, New Orleans, Feb. 1984.

4. Lewis L. Dunnington, *Power To Become* (New York: The Macmillan Co., 1956), 37.

Neglect

How shall we escape, if we neglect so great salvation? (Heb. 2:3).

A writer unknown to me wrote about neglect like this:

> He was going to be all a mortal should be, tomorrow;
> No one should be braver or kinder than he, tomorrow.
> The greatest of workers this man would have been, tomorrow.
> But the fact is, he died and faded from view,
> And all that he left here when living was through—
> Was a mountain of things he intended to do, tomorrow.[1]

There is an old story about a king who sent for his court jester one day, gave him a beautiful cane, and instructed him to keep it until he found a bigger fool than himself.

The years passed and the king grew old. On his deathbed, he wanted to see his old friend the court jester whom he had not seen in many years. Summoning him, the king greeted the old jester warmly and then said sadly, "I am going away."

"And, Sire," the jester asked, "when are you going to return?"

"I shall never return," the king replied, "for I am going to a country far, far away."

"And what provision has your majesty made for his long journey?" the jester asked.

Sadly the king replied, "I have made no preparation at all."

The jester then handed the king the cane and said, "I have kept this cane many years intending to give it to a bigger fool than myself. But I have not found one until today."

"The steamship *Central America*, on a voyage from New York to San Francisco, sprang a leak in mid-ocean. A vessel, seeing her signal of distress, bore down toward her.

"Perceiving her danger to be imminent, the captain of the rescue ship spoke to the *Central America*, asking, 'What is amiss?'

" 'We are in bad repair, and going down. Lie by till morning!'

" 'Let me take your passengers on board NOW,' said the would-be rescuer.

"It was night, and the captain of the *Central America* did not like to transfer his passengers then, lest some might be lost in the confusion, and, thinking that they would keep afloat some hours longer, replied, 'Lie by till morning!'

"Once again the captain of the rescue ship called: 'You had better let me take them now.'

" 'Lie by till morning,' was sounded back through the night.

"About an hour and a half later, her lights were missed! The *Central America* had gone down, and all on board perished, because it was thought they could be saved at another time."[2]

> The road that leads to that mystic land
> Is strewn with pitiful wrecks.
> And the ships that have sailed for its shining strands
> Bear skeletons on their decks,
> It is farther at noon than it was at dawn,
> And farther at night than at noon.
> Oh, let us beware of that land down there—
> The Land of Pretty Soon!
>
> —Author Unknown

1. Charles L. Allen, *Roads To Radiant Living* (Old Tappan, N. J.: Fleming H. Revell, Co., 1961), 37.

2. Walter B. Knight, *Knight's Master Book of New Illustrations* (Grand Rapids, Mich.: Wm. B. Eerdmans Publishing Co., 1956), 519. Used by permission.

Peace

And the peace of God, which passeth all understanding, shall keep your hearts and minds through Christ Jesus (Phil. 4:7).

New Mexico pastor Norm Boshoff told the following story from his pulpit one Sunday.

Eric Barker was a Christian missionary from Great Britain who spent more than fifty years in Portugal, often serving under adverse and dangerous conditions.

During World War II, the situation in Portugal was so tense that Barker was advised to send his wife and eight children to England for safety. His sister and her three children were also evacuated on the same ship. Barker remained behind. He would come later after he had completed some necessary tasks.

The Sunday morning following his family's departure, Barker stood before his congregation and said: "I've just received word that all my family has arrived home safely." He proceeded then with the service as usual.

Later, Barker's congregation learned what he meant by saying that his family had arrived home safely. Just before he went into the worship service, he had received a telegram informing him that a submarine had torpedoed the ship and everyone on board had been lost.

But Barker knew they were all Christians and the knowledge that his family was at peace with the Lord in heaven enabled him to have peace in his heart during the most trying experience of his life.[1]

On January 8, 1815, Tennessean Andrew Jackson, a major general in the United States Army, successfully defended New Orleans. He posted his frontier riflemen behind cotton bales and systematically cut down the enemy as they tried to storm his position.

But the Battle of New Orleans was fought after the peace treaty had already been signed in Europe. Because of the slowness of communications, neither the British army nor the American army knew the war was over.

The Battle of New Orleans was the only spectacular success won by an American army during the entire War of 1812. As a result, Andrew Jackson became a national hero which certainly helped his successful run for the Senate and later his election as the president of the United States.[2]

The unsaved sinner is at war with God, but peace has been made through the shed blood of Jesus. All the sinner has to do is accept it.

Dr. F. Townley Lord was a president of the Baptist World Alliance. Speaking to the Alliance on one occasion, Lord told about some of his experiences in the Second World War.

He said he had been a warden during the war with the responsibility to see that a nearby bomb shelter was open when it was needed. Lord said they had a piano down in the shelter and a good pianist to play it.

One night when they were in the bomb shelter, Lord noticed two young American soldiers and their dates among those seeking shelter. Holding his hand up for silence, Lord told the four young people to come up to the piano and sing a song.

After a bit of hesitation they came to the piano, pushed aside the popular song the group had been singing, opened the hymnbook and began to sing, "Standing On The Promises Of God."

Dr. Lord said that after the quartet had sung, he led the group in prayer. Lord told the Alliance: "I have never been in a church service where the presence of the Holy Spirit was more evident."

In the midst of war, with bombs falling all around them, four young people sang about the peace of God "that passeth all understanding."

Norman Vincent Peale, in his book *The Amazing Results of Positive Thinking*, told a marvelous story about peace in the midst of death and danger.

Peale said that on a visit to Belgium after World War II he went to

Breendonk, located midway between Antwerp and Brepptwpx. During the war, Breendonk had been a notorious prison in which the Nazis had incarcerated loyal, patriotic Belgians who had resisted the invaders.

The Nazis had treated the Belgians like animals, keeping them in miserable little cells, torturing them and trying to crush their spirits. But the prisoners kept up their courage even when times were the most difficult.

After having walked through one of the dark, dismal passageways of the former prison, Peale said he asked his guide: "How could they stand it? How could they stand up under the terrible stress of trying to survive in this horrible place?"

The guide told Peale to follow him and he would show Peale how they survived. Taking Peale back into one of the darkest cells of the prison, the guide showed Peale a crude outline of a man's face that had been carved on the stone wall of the cell.

"When things were the hardest and our people were about to give up because they thought they could stand it no more, they would come in here," the guide said. "They would put their hands on the face of Jesus to remind themselves that they were not alone."

Continuing, the guide told Peale that one night the Nazis came and took away the guide's father and they never saw him again. They learned after the war that he had been imprisoned at Breendonk and, though they couldn't be sure, they felt probably he had died there.

"My father was a devout Christian," the guide said. "We were told that often he came here to place his hand over the face of Jesus."[3]

1. Author unknown; told in the pulpit of Hoffmantown Baptist Church, Albuquerque, N. M., by Pastor Norm Boshoff.

2. Lowell Thomas, *The Vital Spark—101 Outstanding Lives* (Garden City, N. Y.: Doubleday & Co., 1959), 341.

3. Norman Vincent Peale, *The Amazing Results of Positive Thinking* (Englewood Cliffs, N. J.: Prentice-Hall Inc., 1959), 124-125.

Prayer

And he said unto them, When ye pray, say. . . (Luke 11:2).

Huckleberry Finn said prayer doesn't work! Mark Twain has young Huck saying:

> Miss Watson she took me into the closet and prayed, but nothing come of it. She told me to pray every day, and whatever I asked for I would get it. But it warn't so. I tried it. Once I got a fishline but no hooks. It warn't any good to me without hooks. I tried for hooks three or four times, but somehow I couldn't make it work. By and by, one day, I asked Miss Watson to try for me, but she said I was a fool. She never told me why, and I couldn't make it out no way. . . . I says to myself, if a body can get anything they pray for, why don't Deacon Winn get back the money he lost on pork? Why can't the widow get back her silver snuff box that was stole? Why can't Miss Watson fat up? No, says I to myself, there ain't nothing in it.[1]

Of course, humorist Mark Twain, with tongue in cheek, put these words in Huck's mouth. But prayer works and millions of us know it.

When former United States President Ulysses S. Grant lay dying with cancer at Mount McGregor, New York, he was visited by General O. O. Howard who was known among the Union soldiers as the "Christian Soldier." As he and Grant talked about battles they had fought and won, Grant interrupted Howard with the urgent request: "Tell me, Howard, what you know about prayer?"[2]

What do we Christians know about prayer? We probably don't know as much as we should, but we know this for a fact: prayer works.

The Confederate soldier Stonewall Jackson believed in it. An officer complained to General Jackson one day about some soldiers in camp who were making a noise in their tent. When Jackson asked what the soldiers were doing, the officer replied that they were praying and singing. And Jackson replied, "God forbid that praying should be an unusual noise in this camp."

Early American missionary Adoniram Judson believed in it. "Be resolute in prayer," he wrote. "Make any sacrifice to maintain it."

Dwight L. Moody believed in it. "Every great movement of God can be traced to a kneeling figure," he said.

Evangelist George Whitefield believed in it. The famous English evangelist who helped the Wesleys found the Methodist Church, wept, "O Lord, give me souls or take my soul!"

Martin Luther believed in it. In his defense at the Diet of Worms, Luther cried out, "Stand by me, Thou True, Eternal God!"

The American missionary to the Indians, David Brainerd, believed in it. See him there, kneeling in the snow of New England, praying for the salvation of the Indians.

American evangelist Charles Finney believed in it. There he kneels in a hayloft in the middle of the winter, wrapped up in a buffalo robe, praying all night.

Englishman George Muller believed in it. He knelt by his chair day and night and prayed England's orphanage system into existence.

Dr. Wyatt Hunter whom I followed as pastor of the First Baptist Church of McComb, Mississippi, served the church for thirty years and was then named pastor emeritus. A benedictory prayer which he used repeatedly was much loved by his congregation:

Now may the grace of God, bright like the light
When the morning dawneth, and gentle as the dew
When the eventide falleth, be and abide with you
Today and tomorrow and forever more.
Amen and Amen.

A story told by Benjamin P. Browne about evangelist Dwight L. Moody is a great testimony to the power of prayer.

"Invited by the pastor, Mr. Lessey, to take his pulpit on a Sunday, Moody found the atmosphere frosty and dead. But at the evening service there was a startling change in the congregation, for the atmosphere was charged with the lively Spirit of God.

"When Moody gave his invitation, people stood all over the church. He had never seen such an overwhelming response. Concluding that the people had misunderstood him, to clarify his meaning, Moody asked that only those who wanted to make a definite decision for Christ meet him in the inquiry room. People overcrowded the room. Many stood outside. Then he asked all who were seriously bent on becoming Christians to return the next night. So many came that Moody preached for ten days, and over four hundred actually joined the church.

"Moody knew that only prayer could explain such [a] phenomenon. Investigation revealed two devout praying sisters in the church, one of whom was bedridden. The sick one, instead of bemoaning her misfortune, decided that she was not helpless; she would devote her life to prayer for revival in their church. The sisters read of Moody's work in America and prayed that God would send him from America to their church. And this bold prayer was answered. When the sick one had asked her sister, 'Who preached at church this morning?' her companion exclaimed, 'Mr. Moody from America. Our prayers have been answered.'

"Moody's son affirmed that it was this revival that decided the evangelist to return with Sankey and open his campaigns which had astonishing and long-lasting results in England, Scotland, and Ireland."[3]

1. Gaston Foote, *Living in Four Dimensions* (Old Tappan, N. J.: Fleming H. Revell Company, 1953), 83-84. Permission for *Huckleberry Finn* quote requested from publisher Harper & Bros.

2. Clarence Macartney, *Macartney's Illustrations* (New York and Nashville: Abingdon-Cokesbury Press, 1945), 267.

3. Benjamin P. Browne, *Illustrations For Preaching* (Nashville: Broadman Press, 1977), 76-77.

Pride

. . . And the pride of life (1 John 2:16).

Between the towns of Weehawken and Hoboken, N.J., overlooking the Hudson River, there is a stone monument erected to the memory of Alexander Hamilton: "Here on July 11, 1804, Alexander Hamilton fell in a duel with Aaron Burr."

Alexander Hamilton and Aaron Burr were political enemies. Burr killed Hamilton, but it was in fact pride that killed Hamilton.

Alexander Hamilton was the first United States secretary of the treasury. Aaron Burr was vice-president of the United States from 1801 to 1805, under President Thomas Jefferson. Burr's political career ended suddenly when, as vice-president, he killed Alexander Hamilton.

Twice Burr ran for the presidency of the United States—1796 and 1800. In 1800 he and Jefferson tied and the U. S. House of Representatives had to take thirty-six ballots before it chose Jefferson over Burr. And Hamilton used his influence to see that Burr was defeated.

Vice-President Burr ran for governor of New York in 1804. Again, he lost due to the successful maneuvering of Alexander Hamilton. Burr then challenged Hamilton to a duel and the men faced each other on July 11, 1804 at Weehawken, N.J. With one shot, Burr fatally wounded Hamilton. Both New Jersey and New York grand juries indicted Burr for murder.

But the point is this: Hamilton didn't have to die. And Burr didn't have to kill him. Blame pride!

Hamilton was a Christian and dueling was abhorrent to him. When Burr challenged Hamilton his first inclination was to refuse. But Hamilton was afraid that if he did, his future political career and usefulness would be hindered. So rather than doing what he knew was right, Hamilton yielded to what he felt was the pressure of the crowd to conform and he died on the very spot where his son had died a year before.[1]

And Burr, stung by defeat, and disappointment, determined to get even with Hamilton for hindering him politically. So, driven by pride he killed both his career and Hamilton.

Author Halford Luccock says that at the exit of the National Gallery of Art in London there is a large receptacle. When the doorman was asked one day how the receptacle was used, he replied: "That's where the art students drop their conceit as they go out!"

On December 2, 1804, Napoleon was to be crowned emperor of France and he had Pope Pius VII brought to Paris to preside over the coronation cermonies. The Pope was to place the crown on Napoleon's head. But at the last moment, Napoleon changed the proceedings. Grabbing the crown from the Pope's hands, Napoleon crowned himself.

1. *World Book Encyclopedia* and Clarence E. Macartney, *Macartney's Illustrations* (New York and Nashville: Abington-Cokesbury Press, 1945), 113.

Redeem / Redemption

Christ hath redeemed us from the curse of the law (Gal. 3:13).

Redeem: "To redeem, i.e. by payment of a price, from the power of another, to ransom, buy off."[1]

—Joseph H. Thayer

In his volume titled *The Pastoral Epistles in the Greek New Testament*, Kenneth S. Wuest wrote:

> There are three words in the N.T., translated "redeem," which tell the story of the Cross. The first is *agorazo,* "to buy a slave in the market place" (1 Cor. 6:20; 2 Pet. 2:1, Rev. 5:9). The slave market is this earth. All the unsaved are slaves of sin and Satan. Our Lord paid the penalty for sin at the Cross. Those who trust in His blood, belong to Him as His bondslaves. The second is *exagorazo,* "to buy off, to buy up," thus, "to buy out of the slave market" (Gal. 3:13; 4:5). The saved are never to be put up for sale in any slave market again. They belong to the Lord Jesus forever. The third is *lutroo,* "to set free by the payment of a ransom" (Titus 2:14, 1 Peter 1:18). The Lord's slaves are set free from sin and their old master Satan, to experience in their lives, that for which God created them, fellowship with and service to God.[2]

The amount paid for an item reveals its value. The price paid may not reveal the true value, but it reveals the value put on it by the person who bought it.

Donald Grey Barnhouse wrote that *The London Times* used to publish the prices paid for art objects sold from all over the world. If a picture were sold in New York, London, Rome, or Paris, the *Times* would know about it and print the price, he said.

Barnhouse said, suppose we heard a clerk speak about a picture that sold for $25 and another one that sold for $600,000. The price paid would tell us a lot about the picture. We could be sure that the $25 picture didn't amount to too much—perhaps a sunset or a tree painted by an amateur artist.

But the $600,000 picture would probably be a lot different. Maybe it was painted by Reubens, Rembrandt, Millet, or Michelangelo.

But only the person who paid for the picture could really tell what it was worth. If it was worth $600,000 to him, and he was willing to pay that much for the picture, then that's the value of the picture.

So it is with the cross and our redemption. The price that was paid at Calvary to redeem us tells us what we are really worth to God.[3]

And John 3:16 tells us what that price was.

Abraham Lincoln signed the Emancipation Proclamation January 1, 1863. The Proclamation stated: "All persons held as slaves within any State, or designated part of a State, the people whereof shall then be in rebellion against the United States, shall be then, thenceforward, and forever free. . . ." In the South, at that time, there were 3,204,000 slaves, valued at half a billion dollars.

The Proclamation was brought to Mr. Lincoln at noon on January 1, 1863, by Secretary of State William Henry Seward and his son, Frederick.

The document, which had not been unrolled by Seward, was placed on a table before Mr. Lincoln. Mr. Lincoln picked up a pen, dipped it in ink, unrolled the manuscript, and was about to affix his signature to the appropriate place. He hesitated.

Laying the pen down, Lincoln hesitated a few minutes before he picked up the pen and said to Seward: "I have been shaking hands since nine o'clock this morning, and my right arm is almost paralyzed. If my name ever goes into history it will be for this act, and my whole soul is in it. If my hand trembles when I sign the Proclamation, all who examine the document hereafter will say, 'He hesitated.' "

Having rested his hand a few minutes, Lincoln then wrote firmly across the Proclamation, "Abraham Lincoln."

Looking up at Seward, he smiled and said, "That will do."[4]

At Calvary, with the crimson ink of His own blood, Christ signed our Emancipation Proclamation setting us free from sin and its eternal curse. That His heart was in what He did was shown by the way He died.

In their book *The People's Almanac*, David Wallechinsky and Irving Wallace tell about strange insurance policies sold by Lloyd's of London.

The earliest records of Edward Lloyd of London, the founder of the company, showed up in 1688. He died in 1713. But the company he founded has written some unique policies across the years: a "love" insurance policy that was to pay $100,000 if the model of a certain photographer married; a policy insuring against worry lines developing on a model's face; $3,019,400 paid when the *Titanic* sank in 1912; and $5.6 million-plus paid when the *Andrea Doria* was sunk in 1956 off the coast of Nantucket Island when it collided with a freighter.

Also, Lloyd's paid $1,463,400 after the San Francisco earthquake of 1906. They offered a $22,400 policy—with a premium costing $74—in case someone was killed by a falling Russian "sputnik" satellite; a policy for a golfer who wanted insurance against his opponent making a hole-in-one; a policy that would protect a church in case its picnic got rained out; and another policy against having twins.

There's more. Betty Grable's legs were insured for $250,000; Jimmy Durante's nose was insured for $140,000; and Jose Greco, the noted flamenco dancer, had his trousers insured against splitting for $980 a pair.

They also insured dancer Fred Astaire's legs for $650,000, and movie comics Bud Abbott and Lou Costello had a policy for $250,000 insuring against their having a disagreement for five years.

But Lloyd's backed out when an acrobat, who hung by her back teeth in her act, wanted her teeth insured.[5]

But there is nothing strange about the kind of spiritual insurance redemption through the shed blood of Christ gives over the power and penalty of sin when a repenting, believing sinner accepts Jesus as his/her Savior. About this Paul wrote: "Christ hath redeemed us from the curse of the law, being made a curse for us: for it is written, Cursed is everyone that hangeth on a tree" (Gal. 3:13).

1. Joseph Henry Thayer, *A Greek-English Lexicon of the New Testament* (New York: American Book Co., 1889), 221.

2. Kenneth S. Wuest, *The Pastoral Epistles in the Greek New Testament* (Grand Rapids, Mich.: Wm. B. Eerdmans Publishing Co., 1954), 196. Used by permission.

3. Donald Grey Barnhouse, *Let Me Illustrate* (Westwood, N. J.: Fleming H. Revell, 1967), 262.

4. G. B. F. Hallock, *5000 Best Modern Illustrations* (New York: George Doran Company, 1927), 445-446.

5. David Wallechinsky and Irving Wallace, *The People's Almanac* (Garden City, N. Y.: Doubleday & Company, Inc., 1975), 352-353.

Repent / Repentance

Repent ye: For the kingdom of heaven is at hand (Matt. 3:2).

The late Presbyterian minister Clarence E. Macartney wrote about the penitent thief on the cross by the side of Jesus: "The thief and brigand on the cross has stolen horses, jewels, money, children; he has spoiled and plundered caravans. But now he steals heaven. He picks the lock of the gate of heaven with the key of repentance."[1]

Robinson Crusoe author Daniel Defoe, as a young man, ran away from home and went to sea. His mother wept out of a broken heart and his father protested, but young Defoe was determined. On his first voyage, he was shipwrecked and barely escaped with his life. Although he saw the foolishness and sinfulness of his actions, he was ashamed to go back home because he was afraid his friends would make fun of him. With that background, Defoe wrote that people are not ashamed of sin, but they are ashamed to repent.[2]

Theologian Augustus H. Strong wrote: "Repentance is that voluntary change in the mind of the sinner in which he turns from sin."

Roy Angell gave a good illustration of repentance in his book *Shields of Brass*.

During the First World War, Angell wrote, a widowed mother lost her only son and her husband. She was especially bitter because her neighbor, who had five sons, lost none.

One night while her grief was so terribly severe, she had a dream. An angel stood before her and said, "You might have your son back again for ten minutes. What ten minutes would you choose? Would you have him back as a little baby, a dirty-faced little boy, a schoolboy just starting to school, a student just completing high school, or as the young soldier who marched off so bravely to war?"

The mother thought a few minutes and then, in her dream, she told the angel she would choose none of those times.

"Let me have him back," she said, "when as a little boy, in a moment of anger, he doubled up his fists and shook them at me and said, 'I hate you! I hate you!'"

Continuing to address the angel, she said: "In a little while his anger subsided and he came back to me, his dirty little face stained with tears, and put his arms around me. 'Momma, I'm sorry I was so naughty. I promise never to be bad again and I love you with all my heart.'"

"Let me have him back then," the mother sobbed, "I never loved him more than at that moment when he changed his attitude and came back to me."[3]

The late J. Earl Mead, the dean of Southern Baptist religious educators, told a story by Dr. T.W. Ayers that well illustrates the need for repentance.

Ayers, the first Southern Baptist medical missionary, told about an old Chinese woman who came to him one day to have him examine a growth on her head. She wanted the growth removed, but Dr. Ayers said that before he could do anything he had to have answers to some questions.

The doctor asked the woman three questions: "Does it hurt?" "Is it growing?" and "Does it inconvenience you?"

And the woman answered "No" to each of the questions.

Then Dr. Ayers told the woman that he did not believe doing the operation was wise or necessary.

"But," the old Chinese woman replied in a disappointed tone, "I am going to see Jesus before very long, and I don't want to meet him with this blemish on my head."

There is only one way that the blemishes of our sins and failures can be removed from us. Repentance is the only way, and not even God can do it any other way.[4]

Repentance is confessing, "I have sinned," and turning from it. The late R. G. Lee wrote in his book *The Must of the Second Birth*:

> King Pharaoh, who lived as though he had been nursed on the tiger milk of cruelty, said: "I have sinned." Achan, greedy for gold and garments, said: "I have sinned." King Saul, his heart stubborn and in rebellion against the will of God, said: "I have sinned." David, staking his crown for a woman's caress, said, in contrition: "I have sinned."
>
> The Prodigal, back from the hog trough, said to his father: "I have sinned." Judas Iscariot, ridden with the devils of remorse, throwing down the thirty pieces of silver as though they were hissing serpents or burning coals of fire, said, "I have sinned." Peter, after a fruitless night of fishing, saw two ships filled to the sinking point with fishes, and we read: "I am a sinful man, O Lord." Paul spoke of himself as the chief of sinners (1 Timothy 1:15).[5]

The late Carlyle Marney affirmed that sin is called by various names: In theology it is called depravity; in history it is called cruelty and wickedness; in religion it is called sin; in ethics it is called evil; in philosophy it is called the problem of the origin and existence of evil; in psychology it is called egocentricity; and in life itself it is called waste of personality.[6]

But by whatever name man's sin may be called, there is only one answer to it: repentance.

1. Clarence Edward Macartney, *Macartney's Illustrations* (New York and Nashville: Abingdon-Cokesbury Press, 1945), 390.

2. Ibid., 303.

3. Roy Angell, *Shields of Brass* (Nashville: Broadman Press, 1965), 70-71.

4. J. Earl Mead, *With God In The Heights* (Nashville: Broadman Press, 1972), 58.

5. R. G. Lee, *The Must Of The Second Birth* (Westwood, N. J.: Fleming H. Revell Co., 1959), 114-115. Permission requested.

6. Carlyle Marney, *Faith In Conflict* (New York and Nashville: Abingdon Press, 1957), 49.

Resurrection/Easter

For the trumpet shall sound, and the dead shall be raised incorruptible, and we shall be changed (1 Cor. 15:52).

G. Campbell Morgan, the noted preacher whose books line the shelves of many preachers' libraries, wrote about a man who was buried in Italy many years ago. An arrogant agnostic, he was especially critical of the Christian faith.

Morgan says that the man had given instructions preceding his death that when he was buried a slab of granite weighing many tons should be placed over his grave so there would be no chance of his body rising if ever there was a resurrection day. Upon his death, his instructions were carried out and the huge granite slab was lowered over his grave.

But in the process of preparing the grave, a bird flying overhead must have dropped an acorn seed into the grave before the granite slab was laid. In time, the acorn sprouted and a little green oak shoot peeked over the side of the granite slab. The years passed and the slip of a tree grew into a mighty oak splitting the granite slab down the middle.

In telling a similar story—perhaps an adaptation of the one told by Morgan—J. Ralph Grant, pastor emeritus of First Baptist Church, Lubbock, Texas, wrote that a king built a beautiful mausoleum in which his dead body was to be placed. Furthermore, he gave instructions that the words, "Sealed Forever," should be engraved over the top of the mausoleum.

When the king died, his friends placed the king's body inside, but unnoticed by them an acorn also fell into the vault.

The seed sprouted and grew. After several years a giant oak grew out of the grave splitting the mighty slab bearing the not-so-eternal inscription, "Sealed Forever."

Easter means that no grave is sealed forever! If a sprouting acorn can split a granite slab covering a grave, what do you suppose the shout of the archangel and the blowing of the trumpet will do?

Soon a day of rest is coming when Jesus will rock us to sleep in His bosom. But there is also coming a "getting up" day when the Heavenly Father shall whisper in our ear: "Son, Daughter, it's time to get up."

Sir Walter Raleigh (1552?-1618) was an English soldier, explorer, writer, and businessman.

Raleigh is famous for his gallantry to Queen Elizabeth I. In 1581, Raleigh was visiting Queen Elizabeth at her court when, out walking one day, they came to a large mud puddle. As everybody knows, Raleigh removed his coat and placed it over the puddle for the queen to walk on.

More than likely, the story is not true. But it is true that he was Queen Elizabeth's favorite and she gave him a 12,000-acre estate in Ireland. It was on that land that he first planted the potato in 1596.

Raleigh fell into the disfavor of the queen when he married one of her maids-of-honor. To redeem himself with the queen, he traveled to Guyana in South America to search for Eldorado, a legendary land of gold, but the expedition failed.

Possibly you have seen the Tower of London in which James I imprisoned Raleigh after the death of Elizabeth in 1603. There in the Tower of London Raleigh lived for twelve years. Released in 1616, he made another trip to South America to search for gold, being explicitly commanded by the king not to attack the Spaniards. But his men disobeyed and attacked the Spaniards, and when Raleigh returned to London he was sentenced to death for disobeying orders.

He met his fate calmly, even joking with his executioner. Raleigh laid his head upon the chopping block, and gave the signal for the ax to fall.[1]

After Raleigh was beheaded, they found his Bible in the Tower of London in which he had written his epitaph the night before his death:

> Even such is time, that takes in trust
> Our youth, our joys, our all we have

> And pays us but with age and dust;
> Who in the dark and silent grave,
> When we have wandered all our ways,
> Shuts up the story of our days.
> But from this earth, this grave, this dust,
> My God shall raise me up, I trust![2]

In his book *Letter To The Seven Churches and Other Sermons*, Lubbock, Texas, minister J. Ralph Grant wrote:

> The resurrection takes the sting out of death. It brings comfort in the hour of sorrow. It gives hope in the hour of parting. Perhaps you have stood by the grave of a loved one who has fallen asleep in the Lord and there you were comforted as the minister quoted the words, "I am the resurrection and the life: he that believeth in me though he were dead yet he shall live in me." For many years the southern tip of Africa was called the Cape of Storms. The waters about the cape were dreaded by sailors. In fact, sailors shunned those turbulent waters, but one day Vasco De Gama of Portugal successfully sailed around the tip of Africa and came back. It was not so bad after all. So the name was changed from the "Cape of Storms" to "Cape of Good Hope." Now the grave was a cape of storms until Jesus came and arose from the dead. Now for the believer it is a cape of good hope.[3]

Michael Faraday, an English chemist and physicist who was a devout Christian, was born in 1791 and died in 1867. Faraday discovered the principle of electromagnetic induction which is the basis for the electric generator and the electric motor.

One day a workman who was helping Faraday knocked a little silver cup into a jar of strong acid. The cup was quickly destroyed. But Faraday put some chemicals into the jar and in a moment the silver which had disintegrated settled to the bottom. Faraday quickly retrieved it.

The shapeless mass of silver was then sent to a silversmith and the cup was restored as shining, beautiful, and bright as ever.[4]

If Faraday and the silversmith could do that to the dissolved silver cup, cannot God give us a new body on the resurrection morning?

Walter B. Knight relates a story told by Arthur Brisbane about a procession of grieving little caterpillars carrying the remains of a cocoon to the caterpillar cemetery. Sad, disconsolate, weeping, and clothed in funeral garb, the little creatures carry the cocoon along to the cemetery while all the time above their heads flutters a magnificent Monarch butterfly of incomparable beauty![5]

1. *World Book Encyclopedia.*

2. Clarence E. Macartney, *Macartney's Illustrations* (New York and Nashville: Abington-Cokesbury Press, 1945), 118.

3. J. Ralph Grant, *Letters To The Seven Churches and Other Sermons* (Grand Rapids, Mich.: Baker Book House, 1962), 87. Used by permission.

4. Walter P. Knight, *Knight's Master Book of New Illustrations* (Grand Rapids, Mich.: William B. Eerdmans Publishing Co., 1956), 560.

5. Ibid., 563.

6. Carlyle Marney, *Faith in Conflict* (New York and Nashville: Abingdon Press, 1957), 49.

Sacrifice

For with such sacrifices God is well pleased (Heb. 13:16).

In the Alamo in San Antonio, Texas, there is a plaque on one wall that spells out the sacrifice made for Texas freedom:

> It was here that a gallant few, the bravest of the brave, threw themselves between the enemy and the settlements, determined never to surrender nor retreat. They redeemed their pledge to Texas with the forfeit of their lives. They fell the chosen sacrifice to Texas freedom.

Leslie J. Tizard illustrates the sacrifice of Christ for us in a brief note about pioneer British physician Jonathan Hall Edwards:

> But the awareness of what Christ had done for all would not have had such a constraining power if there had not been at the heart of it an intensely personal experience. You may be moved by the story of Jonathan Hall Edwards, one of the pioneers of X-rays, who, working in the city of Birmingham, lost his fingers, his hands, his arms in his efforts to relieve the sufferings of humanity. You are filled with admiration for such self-sacrifice. Yet you are not made humble and grateful as you would be if somebody endured such agony and mutilation in an heroic attempt to relieve your pain or save your life. You cannot be moved to the depths while you think only abstractly or in general terms. It was the deep conviction that "the Son of God loved me and gave Himself up for me" which evoked Paul's gratitude and made him a preacher of the Gospel undaunted by hardships and persecutions.[1]

In the fall of 1812, missionary Harriet Atwood Newell and her husband, Samuel, were on their way to the island of Mauritius near Madagascar. They planned to settle on Mauritius and do missionary work for Jesus. Samuel Newell was a member of the "Haystack Group" in which America's modern mission movement was born.

The Newells did more than pray about missions; they committed themselves to go as missionaries.

On their way to Mauritius, far out on the Indian Ocean, Harriet gave birth to a little baby girl. For a few days the hearts of the parents were overwhelmed with joy. Then the little gift from heaven went to be with Jesus, and grief wiped away all the joy of the young parents.

After the child's death, Harriet showed the first signs of the fatal disease which had been rapidly consuming her life. In November 1812, Harriet Atwood Newell was buried beneath an evergreen tree at Port Louis to become the first American to give her life for the cause of Jesus in foreign missions.

Harriet's last words were these:

> Tell my dear mother how much Harriet loved her. Tell her to look to God and keep near to him and he will support and comfort her in all her trials. Tell my brothers and sisters, from the lips of their dying sister, that there is nothing but religion worth living for. Tell them, and also my dear mother, that I have never regretted leaving my native land for the cause of Christ.[2]

At the Baptist Meeting House at Malden, Massachusetts, is a memorial tablet dedicated to the memory of Adoniram Judson. Judson and his wife, Ann, were the first missionaries to be sent to foreign soil by an American Missionary Society.

In Memoriam

Rev. Adoniram Judson

Born August 9, 1788

Died April 12, 1850

Malden, His Birthplace

The Ocean, His Sepulchre;

Converted Burmans and the Burman Bible

His Monument,

His Record is on High.

1. Leslie J. Tizard, *Preaching: The Art of Communication* (New York: Oxford University Press, 1959), 23. Used by kind permission of Unwin Hyman Ltd.

2. Ethel Daniels Hubbard, *Ann of Ava* (New York: Missionary Education Movement of the US & Canada, 1913).

Salvation

And Jesus said unto him, This day is salvation come to this house (Luke 19:9).

He was born at Hertfordshire, England, November 26, 1731. He died at East Dereham, England, on April 25, 1800.

His name was William Cowper. Educated at Westminster, he was admitted to the bar in 1754. Poet, writer, hymnologist, Cowper was plagued throughout his life with periods of depression and despondency. On several occasions he attempted suicide, but failed each time. On one of those occasions when he attempted suicide, it was because he discovered he would have to "stand for an examination" if he were to succeed in becoming the clerk of the Journals of the House of Lords. From this ordeal he never fully recovered.

He lived for a while with the Morley Unwin family and was particularly attached to them. But when Mr. Unwin died, Cowper had to move with Mrs. Unwin to Olney where he came under the influence of John Newton. Newton was an extreme Calvinist and the theology of the former slave trader who wrote "Amazing Grace," one of Christendom's best-known hymns, put such an emotional and mental weight on Cowper it made recovering from his breakdown all but impossible.

He and Newton, however, were good friends and published a series of hymns in a little booklet, *Olney Hymns.* But insanity struck again and Cowper had to give up writing for gardening, tending to rabbits, and other simple chores.

In 1771, Cowper made what was probably his greatest contribution to the church. He wrote the immortal hymn text, "There Is A Fountain":

There is a fountain filled with blood
Drawn from Immanuel's veins;
And sinners, plunged beneath that flood,
Lose all their guilty stains.
Dear dying Lamb, thy precious blood
Shall never lose its pow'r
Till all the ransomed church of God
Be saved, to sin no more.

Martin Luther (1483-1546), a catalyst for the Protestant Reformation in Germany, was born into the home of a poor miner. But Luther's father had a strong desire to see his son get a good education. Although Luther planned to be a lawyer, he changed his mind while he was in the university and was ordained a priest in 1507.

According to psychoanalyst Erik H. Erikson, Luther's religious doubts and near-despair during his early years as he studied for the priesthood can be traced back to feelings about his father. His father didn't want Luther to be a priest and Luther felt he had rebelled against his father by forsaking the law for the priesthood. That same conflict was then transferred to his relationship to God. He knew he was under his father's condemnation and felt he was also under God's.

In the monastic life, Luther set himself to do everything he could to save himself from the certainity of hell: more fastings than required; excess penitences; starvation; mortification of his body; detailed confessions of sins both real and imagined but still Luther found no peace for his troubled heart.

But deliverance from the great burden came and he found peace of heart at last. Johann Staupitz, the vicar of the Augustinian order in which Luther was serving, appointed him to teach in the new university at Wittenberg which Elector Frederick the Wise was building. Luther was appointed by Staupitz to lecture on theology and the Bible. He had to set himself anew to study, particularly Paul's Epistles to the Romans and the Galatians.

As he was studying Paul's Epistle to the Romans and feeling that the awful justice of God was likely to fall upon him at any moment, Luther found Paul's comment that sinners "shall live by faith." Suddenly the light flooded Luther's heart as it did the heart of Saul the persecutor on the road to Damascus.

Later Luther wrote:

> Night and day I pondered, then I grasped that the justice of God is that righteousness by which through grace and sheer mercy God justifies us through faith. . . . To me, an unworthy, condemned and contemptible creature, altogether without merit, God of his pure and free mercy has given us in Christ all the riches of righteousness and salvation, so that I am no longer in want of anything except faith to believe that this is so. . . . Thereupon I felt myself to be reborn and to have gone through open doors into paradise.[1]

John Wesley's salvation was also rooted in Paul's Letter to the Romans. John Wesley was the son of Samuel Wesley, the Anglican rector of Epworth in Lincolnshire. In the rectory there John was born on June 17, 1703. He died on March 2, 1791, in London, in his eighty-seventh year. During his lifetime he probably traveled more than 250,000 miles, founded the Methodist Church that had about 175,000 members and 630 lay preachers at the time of Wesley's death.

Between 1735 and 1738, Wesley served as a chaplain in colonial Georgia. He wrote in his journal on January 24, 1738: "I went to America to convert the Indians; but Oh! who shall convert me?"

Wesley returned to England in 1737 feeling he had failed in his missionary work. Back in England he met Peter Bohler, a Moravian preacher. In his presence, Wesley said he felt that he lacked "that faith whereby alone we are saved." On May 24, 1738, while attending a Moravian devotional meeting at Aldersgate, as he listened to the reading of Luther's *Preface to the Epistles to the Romans*, Wesley had a spiritual experience that changed his life.[2]

The experience was so deep and so definite that he could mark the exact time he was born again—"about a quarter before nine," he wrote in his journal:

> While he [i.e. Luther, whose words were being read] was describing the change which God works in the heart through faith in Christ, I felt my

heart strangely warmed. I felt I did trust in Christ alone, for salvation; and an assurance was given me that he had taken away my sins, even mine, and saved me from the law of sin and death.[3]

For generations, preachers have told the story of Big Tom. Originally, the story was preserved by Dr. A. C. Dixon. This version of it was told by the late Dr. R. G. Lee at the Southern Baptist Convention in St. Louis in 1947. It is recorded in R. L. Middleton's book *The Accents of Life.*

Years ago there was a certain school in the mountains of Virginia which no teacher could handle. The boys were so rough that the teachers resigned.

A young, gray-eyed teacher applied, and the old director scanned him, then said, "Young fellow, do you know what you are asking? An awful beatin'! Every teacher we have had for years has had to take it."

He replied, "I'll risk it."

Finally, he appeared for duty. One big fellow, Tom, whispered, "I won't need any help, I can lick him myself!"

The teacher said, "Good morning, Boys! We have come to conduct school, but I confess I do not know how unless you help me. Suppose we have a few rules. You tell me and I will write them on the blackboard.

One fellow yelled, "No stealing!" Another yelled, "On time." Finally ten rules appeared.

"Now," said the teacher, "a law is no good unless there is a penalty attached. What shall we do with the one who breaks them?"

"Beat him across the back ten times without his coat on."

"That is pretty severe, Boys. Are you ready to stand by it?"

Another yell, and the teacher said, "School comes to order!"

In a day or so, "Big Tom" found his dinner was stolen. Upon inquiry the thief was located—a little hungry fellow, about ten. The next morning the teacher announced, "We have found the thief and he must be punished according to your rule—ten stripes across the back! Jim, come up here!"

The little fellow, trembling, came up slowly with a big coat fastened up to the neck and pleaded, "Teacher, you can lick me hard as you like, but please don't make me take my coat off."

"Take that coat off; you helped make the rules."

"O, teacher, don't make me!" He began to unbutton, and what did the teacher behold! Lo, the lad had no shirt on, but strings for bracers, over his little bony body.

How can I whip this child? thought he. *But I must do something if I keep this school.* Everything was quiet as death. "How come you to be without a shirt, Jim?"

He replies, "My father died, and mother is very poor. I have only one shirt to my name, and she is washing that today, and I wear my brother's big coat to keep warm." The teacher with rod in hand, hesitated. Just then, "Big Tom" jumped to his feet and said, "Teacher, if you don't object, I will take Jim's licking for him."

"Very well, there is a certain law that one can become a substitute for another. Are you all agreed?"

Off came Tom's coat, and after five hard strokes the rod broke! The teacher bowed his head in his hands, and thought, *How can I finish this awful task?*

Then he heard the entire school sobbing, and what did he see? Little Jim had reached up and caught Tom with both arms around his neck. "Tom, I am sorry I stole your dinner, but I was awful hungry. Tom, I'll love you till I die for taking my licking for me! Yes, I'll love you forever!"

Sinner friend, you have broken every rule and deserve eternal punishment! But Jesus Christ took your scourging for you, died in your stead, and now offers to clothe you with his garments of salvation. Will you not fall at his feet and tell him you will love and follow him forever? "The wages of sin is death, but the gift of God is eternal life through Jesus Christ our Lord."[4]

1. Walter Russell Bowie, *Men of Fire* (New York, Evanston, and London: Harper & Row, 1961), 120-121.

2. Ibid., 191. Walter Russell Bowie in his book, *Men of Fire*, 191, gives the date as May 25, 1738 and Clyde E. Fant Jr. and William M. Pinson Jr. in *Twenty Centuries of Great Preaching Vol. III*, 5, give the date as May 4, 1738.

3. Ibid., (Bowie) 191.

4. R. L. Middleton, *The Accents of Life* (Nashville: Broadman Press, 1948), 108-109.

Satan / Devil

And he said unto them, I beheld Satan as lightning fall from heaven (Luke 10:18).

Once Thomas Carlyle took Ralph Waldo Emerson through what was at that time a terrible slum in London known as Whitechapel. After seeing those slums, Carlyle asked Emerson if he had any trouble believing in the devil. To believe in the devil all one has to do is see the chaos he has brought and continues to bring to the human race.

Martin Luther was once asked to tell how he overcame temptation.

"Well," the great Luther said, "When Satan knocks at the door of my heart for admittance, the Lord Jesus answers. When Satan asks, 'Does Martin Luther live here?' The Lord Jesus replies, 'He used to, but he has moved out. I live here now.'"

Continuing, Luther said, "When the Devil sees nailprints in the hands of my Savior he immediately flees."

Baptist theologian Herschel H. Hobbs wrote in his book *The Origin of All Things*:

> It is not my purpose to probe the mystery as to the origin of Satan. Since God alone is eternal, it may be assumed that Satan is a created being. Since God's creation was 'good,' it follows that Satan was not originally evil. Some interpreters see Isaiah 14:12-14 and Ezekiel 28:11-19 as references to how he became the evil one. Though these passages were directed to pagan rulers, there are elements which could apply to Satan. Evidently he is a fallen angel, who, out of ambition and pride, sought to overthrow his Creator. He and those who followed him were cast out of heaven.[1]

Hobbs continued:

Regardless of how we explain the evil one, his earthly presence is evident. Among other things, the Bible calls him Satan (adversary), Devil (slanderer), and Apollyon (destroyer). As Satan, he is the adversary of both God and man. As Devil, he slanders God to man (Gen. 3) and man to God (Job 1-2). As Apollyon, he seeks to destroy God, man, and every good. Jesus called him a "murderer" or man-killer, a liar and the father of every lie (John 8:44). He also called him "the prince of this world" (John 12:31). Paul refers to him as "the god of this world" or age (2 Cor. 4:4). He also speaks of him as "the prince of the power of the air, the spirit that now worketh in the children of disobedience" (Eph. 2:2). Revelation 12:9 sums it all up in speaking of him as "the great dragon . . . that old serpent, called the Devil, and Satan, which deceiveth the whole world: he was cast out into the earth, and his angels were cast out with him." From the Greek text, "old serpent" may also be translated "original serpent."[2]

The Devil's Beatitudes or Blessings From Below

Blessed are they who are bored with the minister's mannerisms and mistakes; for they get nothing out of the sermon.

Blessed are they who are not interested in the affairs of the church; for they cause the world to say, "The church is failing."

Blessed are they who gossip; for they cause strife and division which pleases me very much.

Blessed are they who are easily offended; for they soon get angry and quit.

Blessed is he who professes to love God but hates his brother; for he shall be with me forever.

Blessed are the troublemakers; for they shall be called the children of the devil.

Blessed is he who has no time to pray; for he shall be easy prey.[3]

Daniel Defoe, the author of *Robinson Crusoe*, wrote about the devil and his work:

> Wherever God erects a house of prayer,
> The devil always builds a chapel there;

> And 'twill be found upon examination,
> The latter has the largest congregation.[4]

Walter B. Knight writes about the "Virgin's kiss" that was used by the judges of the Spanish Inquisition.

When the religious heretic was arrested, he would be told to kneel and kiss the image of the Virgin Mary. If he did so, the arms of the image would suddenly reach out and wrap themselves around him in a deadly grip. Concealed in the arms of the image would be knives which would pierce the body of the victim.

The devil often traps unsuspecting ones like that, Knight states. Satan has many hidden devices and temptations that he skillfully uses to entrap us. That is why we must follow the admonition of Peter to "Be sober, be vigilant; because your adversary the devil, as a roaring lion, walketh about, seeking whom he may devour" (1 Pet. 5:8).[5]

1. Herschel H. Hobbs, *The Origin Of All Things* (Dallas, Tex.: Word, Inc., 1975), 37-38. Used by permission.

2. Ibid, 38.

3. Donald T. Kauffman, *For Instance* (Grand Rapids, Mich.: Baker Book House, 1972), 93. (Kauffman said the material came from the North Association Women of the American Baptist churches.)

4. G. Curtis Jones, *1000 Illustrations for Preaching and Teaching* (Nashville: Broadman Press, 1986), 157.

5. Walter B. Knight, *Illustrations for Today* (Chicago: Moody Press, 1970), 98.

Scriptures/Bible

All scripture is given by inspiration of God (2 Tim. 3:16).

The Bible is the most unique book known to mankind. It contains 3,566,480 letters, 810,677 words, 31,175 verses, 1,189 chapters and 66 books.

The longest chapter is Psalm 119.

The shortest and middle chapter is Psalm 117. The middle verse is Psalm 118:8. The longest name in the Bible is *Mahershalalhashbaz*, found in Isaiah 8:1.

The word *and* occurs 46,627 times. The word *Lord* appears 1,855 times. The longest verse is Esther 8:9 and the shortest is John 11:35. All the letters of the alphabet except *j* can be found in Ezra 7:21.

Some lovers of the Bible say that Acts 26 is the Bible's finest chapter. The name of God does not appear in Esther.

The Bible contains knowledge, wisdom, the mind of God, the state of man, the way of salvation, the doom of sinners, and the happiness of believers. Its doctrines are holy; its precepts binding; its history is true; and its decisions are immutable. It contains light to guide one and food to support one and comfort to cheer one.

More than forty men participated in writing it over a period of 1,600 years. But it has only one author—the Holy Spirit. The men used by the Holy Spirit to write the sacred Scriptures were doctors, farmers, fishers, kings, shepherds, old, young, rich, poor, learned and unlearned.

Although it deals with the greatest theme known to mankind or God, the Bible's vocabulary is strikingly limited. Only 6,000 different words are used—not much when compared to the 20,000 words used by Shakespeare. The average word in the Bible contains but five letters. But some of these words are the sweetest and most-loved words known to millions: *grace, peace, faith, saved, serve, glory,* and *Jesus!*

It is the traveler's map, the pilgrim's staff, the pilot's compass, and the soldier's sword. It is a gold mine of wealth and health to the soul and contains rivers of immense pleasure. It is given to us in this life to help us be prepared for the next life.[1]

It takes seventy hours and forty minutes to read the Bible as a minister would read it in the pulpit. Reading at an average rate, one can read the Old Testament in fifty-two hours and twenty minutes and the New Testament in eighteen hours and twenty minutes. Those who love the Psalms, can read all 150 of them in no more than four hours and twenty-eight minutes. The gospel of Luke which contains enough divine inspiration to save the world and change every life, can be read in only two hours and forty-three minutes.

The average reader can read the Bible through in a year if he or she will read it for only twelve minutes a day.

Author Robert J. Hastings in his book *A Word Fitly Spoken*, wrote about Abraham Lincoln's love for the Thirty-seventh Psalm.

Joseph R. Sizoo was once pastor of the New York Avenue Presbyterian Church in Washington, D.C. This was the church Abraham Lincoln often attended while he was president.

Sizoo told how moved he was the first time he held the Bible of Abraham Lincoln. It was the Bible Lincoln had heard his mother read when he was only a boy. He had learned by memory many verses his mother had read to him from that old Bible. It is told that this was the only possession Lincoln took with him from Pigeon Creek to the Sangamon River and on to Washington when he was elected president.

Sizoo said he wondered where the old sacred Book would fall open when he picked it up. He said it opened to a page well thumb-marked which gave evidence of having been read many times: "Fret not thyself because of evil doers . . . Trust in the Lord and do good . . . Delight thyself also in the Lord . . . " (Psalm 37:1,3,4).

From the pen of the late R. G. Lee came these tributes to the Bible:

- Martin Luther: "The Bible is the cradle in which Christ lies."
- American patriot Patrick Henry, near death: "Here is a Book, the Bible, worth more than all others that were ever printed; yet it is my misfortune never to have found time to read it."
- George Washington: "It is impossible to govern rightly the world without God and the Bible."
- Woodrow Wilson: "The Bible is the word of life."
- Ulysses S. Grant: "To the influence of the Bible we are indebted for the progress made in true civilization and to this we must look for our guide in the future."
- England's William Gladstone: "The Bible, impregnable rock of the Holy Scripture."
- Scotland's Sir Walter Scott near death: "Bring me the Book. There is but one Book."
- Benjamin Franklin: "Create a firm belief in the Bible is my advice to young men."
- Napoleon: "The soul can never go astray with the Bible for its guide."
- Confederate General Robert E. Lee: "The Bible, a Book in comparison with which, in my eyes, all others are of minor importance, has never failed to give me strength."
- Helen Keller, blind and deaf, said: "Forty years I have loved the Word of God."
- President Andrew Jackson as he was dying: "That Book, Sir, is the rock on which the republic rests."[2]

God's Word survives. It has survived abuse, misuse, rejection, persecution, liberalism, the rise and fall of pagan kingdoms, and continues to bless the hearts of all who read it. It is a good survivor.

To illustrate how the Bible survives, consider the experience of missionary Alexander Duff. A Scotsman and great missionary pioneer of the Church of Scotland, Duff reached Calcutta, India, in 1830, at the age of twenty-four, to begin his missionary service.

Twice on the voyage he suffered shipwreck. In one of the shipwrecks young Duff lost his precious library of 800 volumes. As he and the little group of survivors stood on the seashore looking out across the angry waves that had swallowed his library, he saw a small object bobbing up and down in the water.

Duff waited and watched until the tide brought the object to the shore. It was his Bible. Though he had lost all his other books, his Bible had survived.

John Wesley, the great Anglican preacher who founded the Methodist Church, wrote in the preface to a volume of his sermons which was published in 1746:

> I am a creature of a day, passing through life as an arrow through the air. I am a spirit, come from God and returning to God: just hovering over the great gulf. I want to know one thing—the way to heaven; how to land safe on that happy shore. God Himself has condescended to teach the way. He hath written it in a Book. O! give me that Book![3]

Tulsa, Oklahoma, First Baptist Church Pastor Dr. Warren Hultgren has been a popular preacher for decades. Robert J. Hastings wrote the following story about Hultgren in *The Baptist Program* in January 1978.

> Warren Hultgren, pastor of the First Baptist Church in Tulsa, Oklahoma, talks informally with his radio listeners during the offertory. One morning he shared a unique story about one of his listeners.
>
> It seems that one listener—who attended another church in Tulsa—preferred Hultgren's sermons over those of his own pastor. So he took a transistor radio to the 'other' church where he listened to Hultgren while his own pastor was preaching. So Hultgren just told this little incident over the air. And as the story goes, it shocked this gentleman so much that he stood right up in the church and cried, "Say, he's talking about ME!"[4]

In the Bible, the Heavenly Father talks about me. It's a personal word from Him to me.

When I am lonely, the 23rd Psalm reminds me that "the Lord is my shepherd," and my heart says, "He's talking about me!"

When I walk in the shadows of heartache, the words of Jesus come to me: "I will not leave you comfortless." And my heart sings, "He's talking about me!"

When I lie down to die, the words of Jesus will comfort me: "In my Father's house are many mansions." And my heart will sigh, "He's talking about me!"

English novelist Charles Dickens (1812-1870) well-known for *A Christmas Carol* and *A Tale of Two Cities*, once wrote to his son: "I put a New Testament among your books for the very reason and with the same hopes that made me write an easy account of it when you were a little child—because it is the best book that ever was or ever will be in the world, and because it teaches you the best lessons by which any human creature who tries to be truthful and faithful can possibly be guided."[5]

1. Author unknown (from Fowler's personal file: Bible)

2. R. G. Lee, *Bought By The Blood* (Nashville: Broadman Press, no date), 129-130.

3. Ian Macpherson, *Live Sermon Outlines* (Grand Rapids, Mich.: Baker Book House, 1974), 13.

4. *The Baptist Program*, January 1978, 4.

5. R. L. Middleton, *Don't Disappoint God* (Nashville: Broadman Press, 1951), 89.

Sin

For all have sinned, and come short of the glory of God (Rom. 3:23).

Evangelist Dwight L. Moody said: "Unconfessed sin is unforgiven sin, and unforgiven sin is the darkest, foulest thing on this sin-cursed earth."

College professor Dr. Nat Tracy defined sin as the possession of a nature which has as its chief characteristic rebellion against God. And English preacher Alexander Maclaren wrote:

> The word *to save* means either of two things—to heal from a sickness, or to deliver from a danger. These two ideas of sickness to be healed and of danger to be secured from enter into the Christian use of the word. Underlying it is the implication that the condition of humanity is universally that of needing healing of a sore sickness, and of needing deliverance from an overhanging and tremendous danger. And sin is the sickness, and the issues of sin are the danger. And sin is making myself my centre and my law, and so distorting and flinging out of gear as it were, my relations to God.[1]

Scottish preacher Ian Macpherson wrote about sin:

> Plainly there is something radically wrong with it (the world), a fundamental disharmony, an elemental dislocation, a basic bias toward evil. You can try to account for the fact of sin as you like. You can call it a theological fiction, a pathological state deliberately fomented in the public mind by the salaried representatives of religion with a view to implementing their own ends and securing their own vested interests. You can call it an evolutionary legacy, the moral hangover from our alleged animal ancestry. You can call it "good in the making," "the growing pains of the race," or what you will. The one thing you cannot do is to deny that it has made havoc of God's fair earth. Scripture declares that the havoc is so dreadful that even

an omnipotent God could only save the world by dying for it![2]

There is an old story—whether true I cannot tell—about Leonardo da Vinci who was painting his grand masterpiece "The Last Supper." He was searching for the perfect model for Christ. Someone suggested to da Vinci that he contact a young man who sang in the choir of one of the old churches of Rome. "Ask for Pietro Bandinelli," da Vinci was told. "He is a young man of such pure life and noble countenance that he will make a fine model for Jesus."

Leonardo da Vinci found the young man. He not only possessed a beautiful countenance, but his life was as beautiful and pure as his face. At last da Vinci could complete the painting for he had found the perfect model to sit for Jesus.

After da Vinci had finished painting Jesus, he painted the eleven disciples and considerable time was required for him to finish the painting. When finally he came to paint Judas, da Vinci began to search the city over for someone to sit as a model for Judas. Da Vinci wanted someone whose face was hardened and upon whose features sin had drawn heavy lines.

At last he found his man. He was the perfect model for Judas for he had the marks of a hard and wicked life written across his countenance. When da Vinci asked the man his name, the man replied: "I am Pietro Bandinelli. I also sat some years ago as your Christ."

Da Vinci could not believe it, but there before him was the evidence of what sin does in one's life.

Clarence Cranford wrote about Dr. Oscar Blackwelder who served a church for many years near the Supreme Court Building. Blackwelder pointed out that the marble of which the Supreme Court Building is made is so white it fairly blinds one to look at it under the summer sun. But when it snows, the Supreme Court Building looks gray. Our purest character is a dismal gray compared to the matchless purity and spotless perfection of Jesus Christ.[3]

Oliver Cromwell (1599-1658) ruled England between 1649 and 1658 during what is called the period of the Commonwealth and Protectorate.

He had a large wart on his face and one day when he was having his portrait painted, he said to the portrait artist, "Paint me just as I am, wart and all." That's what the Bible does. It doesn't cover up our sins. It paints us warts and all!

Author Victor Hugo in his story "The Toilers of The Sea," tells about a man thrusting his arm down into a crevice in the sea to pull out a crab. His arm was immediately seized by something strong as steel but as cold as ice. It wound its tentacles around the fisherman's arm and as the man struggled, the thing shot out a second, third, fourth, and fifth tentacle and wound itself around the man's chest.

Sin is like that. One sin is quickly followed by another sin as each tightens its grip upon the sinner. Then there is another sin and another until the sinner is drawn down to destruction and eternal doom.

Sin is not prejudiced. It treats everybody the same—the high and low, the meek and the mighty. Both the greatest people and the sorriest people have been ruined by it.

For example, Henry Ward Beecher (1813-1887) was a great Protestant preacher in the last century. From 1847 until he died in 1887 he was pastor of the Congregationalist Plymouth Church in Brooklyn, New York. Beecher was known and loved by hundreds of thousands of people.

While he was pastor of the Brooklyn church, Beecher was tried for adultery. The woman implicated was Elizabeth Tilton. According to William P. Tuck, writing in James Hightower's book *Illustrating Paul's Letter To The Romans*, Beecher's trial lasted "six months and received more space in the newspaper than any event since the Civil War."

Beecher was found innocent but many of that day believed he was guilty. Both *The New York Times* and *The Louisville Courier-Journal* indicated Beecher was cleared of the charges only because of the huge amount of money spent to clear him and the powerful lawyers who defended him.

It is not our place, at this late date, to pass judgment on Henry Ward Beecher. And whether he was innocent or guilty we cannot tell. But we know this for fact: "All have sinned and come short of the glory of God."[4]

All are tempted and all sin. Look at Shakespeare's broken heros: Macbeth yielded to avarice; Hamlet was defeated by indecision; Othello was overcome by jealousy; and Richard III was shackled by greed.

Look at the broken heroes in the Bible: Adam and Eve were tempted and sinned. Cain killed Abel in a jealous rage. Moses slew the Egyptian. Abraham lied about Sarah being his wife. David committed adultery and murder. King Saul was destroyed by pride. King Herod was brought down by jealousy and fear. Ananias and Sapphira was devoured by greed. Simon Peter was brought down by fear. Judas was destroyed by materialism. And Saul of Tarsus was victimized by hate.

And the list—in the Bible and out of it—is endless.

The late R. G. Lee graphically described sin as follows:

Sin incurs the penalties of spiritual and physical death. Where is relief to be found? In God's forgiveness.

Sin is debt; God's forgiveness and God's acceptance of the crimson coin of Christ's blood the payment for that debt.

Sin is a cloud; God's forgiveness the sun which does away with the cloud.

Sin is stain; God's forgiveness the blood bath which washes the stain away.

Sin is dross; God's forgiveness the fire which burns the dross out.

Sin is darkness; God's forgiveness the light which dispels it.

Sin is a burden; God's forgiveness the removal of it.

Sin is a corpse—the "body of death" (Romans 7:24); God's forgiveness the burial of that corpse in the sea's depth.

Sin is poison; God's forgiveness the antidote.

Sin is captivity; God's forgiveness freedom from captivity.

Sin is a blotted and blurred record; God's forgiveness the erasure of the record.

Sin is death; God's forgiveness Christ's meritorious life substituted for your forfeited life.[5]

1. Alexander Maclaren, *Expositions Of Holy Scripture, John, Jude, and Revelation* (London: Hodder and Stoughton; New York, George H. Doran Co., no date), 88.

2. Ian Macpherson, *The Burden Of The Lord* (New York and Nashville: Abingdon Press, 1960), 24-25. Used by permission

3. Clarence Cranford, *His Life Our Pattern* (Nashville: Broadman Press, 1960), 104.

4. James E. Hightower, *Illustrating Paul's Letters To The Romans* (Nashville: Broadman Press, 1984), 106.

5. Robert G. Lee, *The Sinner's Saviour* (Nashville: Broadman Press, 1950), 4-5.

Sowing / Reaping

Be not deceived; God is not mocked: for whatsoever a man soweth, that shall he also reap (Gal. 6:7).

There is a classic story in R. L. Middleton's book *The Accents of Life* that well illustrates the principle of sowing and reaping. The story, as told by Roy Angell, is unforgettable.

"I am thinking of an old minister whose life was a constant inspiration to all who knew him. There was something so kind and beautiful about his spirit that the words of Jesus often applied to him: 'In whom is no guile.' I think the secret of it all was one of those unforgettable experiences that came to him in his boyhood on the farm.

"In his own words, it was about as follows," Angell said.

I came home to lunch on the run one day, and grabbed my dad around the waist. "The fish are biting in the millpond and all the boys are going fishing after school this afternoon. May I go?" My father's expression was a little pained as he answered haltingly, "I'm sorry, son, but we're planting corn in the bottom land today, and you have to put the beans in."

I countered, "Couldn't I plant them tomorrow?"

"No, son, we can't leave the corn exposed to the crows. We'll have to put the beans in this afternoon. You can go fishing tomorrow, though."

"If I hurry and get through, can I go then?" He smiled and patted my head, "Yes," he said, "when you plant the beans in this bucket you can go."

I flew home from school that afternoon and snatched up the bucket and went down the first row in a trot, dropping two beans in a hill just as Father had directed. When I had finished three rows I seemed to have just as many as when I started. I'd never get rid of them at that rate, so I began dropping three in a hill, and when they still disappeared too slowly, I just dropped little handfuls in a hill. Soon there weren't many left so I dumped them in one hill and went fishing.

I forgot all about those beans until one evening I found Father waiting for me. Very quietly he said, "Let's go down to the bottom land and see how the corn and beans came up." That's the first time I realized those beans would come up just where I had planted them. When we got to the first row, Dad remarked, "They came up fine here, son, two in a corn hill, just like we wanted them." We walked a little further, "They came up extra fine here; three, four, five in a hill." Then he stopped where I had emptied the bucket. You couldn't see a thing but beans, beans, beans.

I knew I deserved a thrashing—instead, my father's arm slipped around my shoulders and he said, "Let's kneel down here; I want to talk to God a little." I'll never forget that prayer: "Father in Heaven, I don't mind losing a crop of beans if you'll just teach my boy that the beans always come up in life. Teach him that he will always reap what he sows."[1]

Augustine, the fourth-century church father, profited immensely from the sowing/reaping principle. Wicked, profligate, wanting nothing of his mother's Savior, Augustine moved from Carthage in north Africa to Milan in Italy. But Monica, his devout mother, continued to pray for her wicked son's salvation. For sixteen years she held on to the prayer promises of the Bible on behalf of her son and at last Augustine was gloriously converted. It seemed for a while that he would never come to Jesus, for the more she prayed and suffered the wilder and more wicked Augustine became. But one day in a garden in Milan, Augustine met Jesus. Augustine said a voice came to him: "Take up and read; take up and read." And as he did, his Bible opened to Romans 13:13-14 and Augustine was "instantly" saved, as he put it.

Many years ago, a barbers' union in Chicago performed a "miracle" for publicity purposes. Advertising a certain brand of soap, the barbers claimed it would do wonders for anyone who used it. To illustrate the power of their soap, they went down on Madison Street, and found the filthiest drunk they could find, took him to a barber shop and cleaned him up. They shaved him, lathered him with their special kind of soap, shampooed him with their soap and took him to a hotel that exclusively used their kind of soap, bought him a new suit and gave him shirts and socks that had been laundered with their special soap.

The barbers then published their good news in the newspaper: "See what we have done. We have made a new man with our soap." Of course the implication was that anyone who bought and used their special soap would also be "remade."

However, about a week later, page 13 of the local newspaper carried this irreverent comment, "The man made over by the barbers' union was found last night on Madison Street—drunk, dirty and disillusioned."[2]

Sinclair Lewis (1885-1951) was an American novelist and the first American to win a Nobel Prize for Literature (1930). A popular writer in the 1920s and 1930s, one of his well-known novels is the tale of a preacher gone wrong named Elmer Gantry.

As a young man, Sinclair Lewis was a cocky, red-haired atheist. He became friends with Dr. William L. Stidger, Kansas City Methodist minister, who invited Lewis to speak one Sunday evening from Stidger's pulpit. Never one to pass up an opportunity to sensationalize things, Lewis accepted and in his speech he held up his watch and boldly proclaimed that there is no God. Then he threw down the gauntlet: "If there is a God, I defy Him to strike me dead in the next two minutes." Lewis then held his watch up and boldly counted off the seconds to see if God would respond.

God didn't respond, for He has His own way of dealing with sinners. Lewis became a successful writer and a heavy drinker and had several breakdowns. His family life was not good. Married and divorced several times, he couldn't even get along with his sons. Most of his last years were spent wandering throughout Europe. He died in Rome, a lonely embittered man and only his secretary was present at his deathbed.

While he was in the hospital during his last illness, not a person came to see him. After he died and his body was sent to the crematorium, not a person attended him on his last journey.[3]

Sinclair Lewis was sixty-six when he died, but he looked more like he was 80. His last words were, "At least let the sun come back."

1. R. L. Middleton, *The Accent of Life* (Nashville: Broadman Press, 1948), 110-111.

2. Adapted from J. B. Fowler's file "Salvation," 145.

3. Benjamin P. Browne, *Illustrations for Preaching* (Nashville: Broadman Press, 1977), 151.

Suffering/Trials

For I reckon that the sufferings of this present time are not worthy to be compared with the glory which shall be revealed in us (Rom. 8:18).

The late Pittsburgh Presbyterian minister Clarence Macartney said that over each of the three great front doors of a magnificent cathedral in Milan, Italy, is an inscription. Over one door there is carved a wreath of roses and beneath the roses the words, "All that which pleases is but for a moment." Over the second door there is carved a cross, and the words, "All that which troubles is but for a moment." But on the great central door are the words, "That only is important which is eternal."[1]

Few Americans have begun with as little and have contributed to life as much as Abraham Lincoln. With less than a year of formal schooling, he struggled through his trials to live successfully. He set in motion the wheels that brought liberty to four million black slaves when he signed the Emancipation Proclamation in January 1863.

John Bunyan suffered miserably in England. For twelve years he languished in Bedford, England's, jail for preaching the gospel. But in those twelve years he gave to the world one of its noblest pieces of literature: *Pilgrim's Progress.*

John Keats, the English poet, was orphaned at fifteen and was dead at twenty-six. He is remembered as the most remarkable of the English romantic poets.

Beethoven was reared in poverty, the son of a drunken father. When Beethoven's mother died, he had to support his brothers and sisters. Then at twenty-eight, deafness began to settle over him like a suffocating blanket. By the time he was fifty-nine, Beethoven could only communicate by writing, but in the quiet world in which he lived he composed masterpieces.

Thomas Edison, who patented more inventions than any man in history, did so in spite of near-deafness. Helen Keller overcame both blindness and deafness to bless millions. Sir Walter Scott rose above his lameness to become Scotland's greatest romantic novelist and his *Ivanhoe* has been read by millions. Benjamin Disraeli suffered through prejudice but became England's only Jewish prime minister.

The noblest advances made in human history have been made by people who lived effectively in spite of their problems.

Life is filled with problems and trials and we will have our share of them. We have to learn how to handle them for we cannot walk out on them like Sam did.

Sam was to have surgery. Everything was ready. Just before they put Sam to sleep, the doctor said, "I think I ought to tell you that nine out of ten people don't survive this operation. Is there anything I can do for you before we put you to sleep?"

"Yes, Doc, there is," Sam said. "Please hand me my hat!"

Many of the great hymns of the faith were written by people who suffered. One of them was Rev. Henry Francis Lyte and his hymn "Abide with Me" has blessed people for generations.

For twenty-four years Lyte was pastor of the little church at Brixham, England. He became ill with tuberculosis and was told by his physician to go to the sunny South of France to rest and recuperate.

After he had conducted his last service in the little church, with deep sadness in his heart he walked one Sunday evening in 1847 down by the seashore thinking about what had been and what might be. Although he did not know it, he was leaving his beloved parish never to return.

As he walked by the seashore on that Sunday evening, he said he heard the "voiceless whisper of the great unseen" and the prayer-hymn was finalized in his mind. The next morning he left to settle in Nice, France, where, some time later, pointing his hand upward he whispered, "Peace! Joy!" and died. He lies buried in the English cemetery at Nice and his grave is marked by a marble cross.

Lyte's hymn is a favorite:

> Abide with me: fast falls the eventide;
> The darkness deepens; Lord, with me abide:
> When other helpers fail, and comforts flee,
> Help of the helpless, O abide with me!
> Swift to its close ebbs out life's little day;
> Earth's joys grow dim, its glories pass away;
> Change and decay in all around I see:
> O Thou who changest not, abide with me!

The master storyteller Roy Angell retold a story written by George Strombeck that appeared several years ago in *Christian Digest.*

Strombeck said he was walking by a jeweler's store one day when he saw a diamond cutter at work. He had a pile of small, brown, ugly stones on a table before him that looked like rocks one could pick up by the side of any brook. Beside the stones was a small machine that consisted of two disks that looked much like dinner plates.

As Strombeck watched, the diamond cutter removed the top of one of the plate-like disks and there inside were six beautiful, glistening diamonds held in place by small clamps. The diamond cutter picked up each diamond and examined it carefully, sprinkled from a box some diamond dust on each stone, snapped each stone back into place and turned on the machine. Strombeck knew that the diamond cutter was polishing and honing the diamonds until they would be fit for the finger of the most elegant lady in town. Strombeck said he learned from that how God pours the diamond dust of His grace upon our lives as we suffer and uses our trials to polish us into diamonds fit for His service.[2]

1. Clarence E. Macartney, *Macartney's Illustrations* (New York and Nashville: Abington-Cokesbury Press, 1945), 352-353.

2. Roy Angell, *Iron Shoes* (Nashville: Broadman Press, 1953), 44-45.

Temptation

Lead us not into temptation (Matt. 6:13).

It is said that Ulysses, of Trojan War fame, when forced to sail past the dangerous rocks of the Sirens, stuffed the ears of his men with wax so they could not hear the Sirens' dangerously seductive music. Ulysses knew that if he or his men yielded to the temptations of the maidens it would mean disaster for them and his ship. But he wanted to hear the Sirens' beautiful music so he had himself lashed to his ship's mast so he would not yield to their seductive call.

But Orpheus, sailing past the same rocks, handled the temptation much better. He played on his lyre and sang so loudly that he drowned out the call of the temptresses. As Orpheus played and sang, his men rowed their ship in time to the music and sailed safely past the temptation.[1]

In his "Epistle to a Young Friend," Scottish poet Robert Burns wrote about temptation:

> But when on life we're tempest driv'n—
> A conscience but a canker—
> A correspondence fix'd wi' Heav'n,
> Is sure a noble anchor!

Clarence Macartney wrote:

> The first temptation in the history of the human race took place in a garden, and with man at peace with the whole animal creation. The temptation of Jesus, the second Adam, took place in a wilderness, where he 'was with the wild beasts.' That contrast between the first temptation and the

temptation of Jesus, one in a garden, the other in a desert, is a picture of the ruin which had been wrought by sin.[2]

In his book *Great Interviews of Jesus*, Macartney also wrote that English painter George Romney (1734-1802) excelled in portraits of women. His best-known model was the beautiful Emma Hart, later Lady Hamilton, at whose feet Admiral Horatio Nelson, England's greatest naval hero, cast away his honor and character.

Romney also succumbed to Emma Hart's beauty and left his wife and two young children for Hart.

During the years of Romney's success, he hardly ever returned home to his wife. But near the end of his life, broken physically and mentally, he went back to her and she lovingly cared for him until he died.

Tennyson, in his poem "Romney's Remorse," describes Mrs. Romney's love for her wayward husband and how she tried to cheer him in his last days.

"Take comfort, you have won the Painter's fame," she says encouragingly. But Romney replies: "The best in me that sees the worst in me, and groans to see it, finds no comfort there."[3]

Some years ago a hearing clinic at Northwestern University ran some experiments on words that are hard to hear. One of the very hard words to hear, they discovered, is the word *no*. However, that's the word Satan must often hear from the Christian.

In Jack London's marvelous book *The Call of the Wild*, Buck, the Newfoundland dog, is the hero.

Buck was stolen from his home in the states and shipped off to Alaska where, no longer a fireside pet, he had to survive as best he could.

His new master made Buck a husky—a trail dog pulling a sled—and he was the best and strongest on the trail. After his master became ill, Buck had more leisure time than he needed and he began to make frequent trips into the forest. At first the trips were brief, but then they became longer and longer. A good hunter, Buck was able to provide for himself when he was away from camp.

But one night while Buck was out in the forest on a hunt, he heard the lonesome howl of a wolf and his bristles stood up and he was ready to fight the wolf which he felt threatened him.

Time passed and Buck became more accustomed to the howl of the wolves. One night when Buck met the wolf that had caused his bristles to rise, there was no battle and little discomfort. Buck and the wolf put their noses together, made a pact with each other, and trotted off into the forest together.

But when daylight came, Buck would always go back home. When his master died, the tie that had held Buck to home was broken, and he began to run with the wild pack and soon he was the wildest wolf of all.

Once Buck had felt threatened by even the howl of a wolf, but the more he was around that which had threatened him, the more comfortable he became with it.

1. Lewis L. Dunnington, *Power to Become* (New York: The Macmillan Co., 1956), 80.

2. Clarence E. Macartney, *Great Interviews of Jesus* (Nashville: Abingdon Press, 1954), 11.

3. Ibid., 21.

Trust

But I trust in the Lord (Phil. 2:24).

Clarence McCartney wrote that Dwight L. Moody's favorite verse was Isaiah 12:2: "Behold, God is my salvation; I will trust, and not be afraid: for the Lord Jehovah is my strength and my song; he also has become my salvation."

Moody said, "You can travel first-class or second-class to heaven. A second-class traveler says, 'What time I am afraid, I will trust.' But the first-class way of traveling says, 'I will trust and not be afraid.' "[1]

> Trust Him when dark doubts assail thee,
> Trust Him when thy strength is small;
> Trust Him when to trust Him simply
> Seems the hardest thing of all.

—Author Unknown

Few people have meant as much to the kingdom of God as did missionary Hudson Taylor (1853-1905). Founder of the China Inland Mission in 1865, Taylor first went to China in 1853.

When Hudson Taylor was in the closing months of his life, he was so weak he could do very little. To a friend he wrote: "I am so weak I cannot work; I cannot read my Bible; I cannot even pray. I can only lie still in God's arms like a little child, and trust."[2]

Among the notable Christian hymns written by Frances Ridley Havergal (1793-1870) were, "Take My Life and Let It Be" and "I Gave My Life For Thee."

The last day of her life, Miss Havergal who was a devout Christian and a faithful reader of the Scriptures, asked one of her friends to read to her the forty-second chapter of Isaiah. It is a great passage which declares in verses 6 and 8:

> I the Lord have called thee in righteousness, and will hold thine hand, and will keep thee, and give thee for a covenant of the people, for a light of the Gentiles. . . . I am the Lord: that is my name: and my glory will I not give to another, neither my praise to graven images.

As the friend came to that special sixth verse and the words, "I the Lord have called thee in righteousness, and will hold thine hand, and will keep thee," Miss Havergal whispered: "Called, held, kept. I can go home on that!"[3]

Jack Finegan told about one of America's great industrialists—James L. Kraft. His food products have been on American grocery shelves for decades and most of us have bought them.

When Kraft started out in Chicago many years ago, he sold his cheese products out of the back of a horse-drawn wagon. He and his horse, Paddy, weren't doing so well and Kraft was about to go broke. He worked hard during the day and stayed up half the night trying to figure out what to do, but things continued to go downhill.

One day as Paddy was pulling the wagon down one of Chicago's streets, Kraft asked, "What are we doing wrong, Paddy? What's the matter with us?"

Kraft suddenly realized he had been trying to build his business without divine help. From that moment, he determined to let God become his business partner.

Beginning with a sixty-five-dollar investment, Kraft built his business into a multi-billion-dollar business which is known all over the world. In later years when Kraft told the story of his life and recounted his success, he always told how things turned around when he started trusting God and listening to Him.[4]

1. Clarence Macartney, *Macartney's Illustrations* (New York and Nashville: Abingdon-Cokesbury Press, 1945), 401.

2. Walter B. Knight, *Knight's Master Book of New Illustrations* (Grand Rapids, Mich.: Wm. B. Eerdmans Publishing Co., 1956), 703. Used by permission.

3. Ibid., 705.
4. Jack Finegan, *At Wit's End* (Richmond, Va.: John Knox Press, 1963), 14.

Unbelief

And he marvelled because of their unbelief (Mark 6:6).

Clarence Macartney wrote about the unbelief of Mark Twain.

Mark Twain (1835-1910) was one of our best-known American authors and humorists. His real name was Samuel Langhorne Clemens. He is best known for his novels, *The Adventures of Tom Sawyer* and *The Adventures of Huckleberry Finn*.

Mark Twain married Oliva Langdon. She was a simple and devout Christian, but he was not a believer. For a while after they were married, they had prayer at meals and read the Bible each day. But this was soon given up. According to a conversation she had with her sister, Oliva said she had given up some of her religious beliefs. Her faith was shaken by people, places, and philosophies to which she was exposed as she traveled the world with her husband.

Oliva's pet name for her husband was, "Youth." Their only son, Langdon, died in infancy and two of their three daughters—Susy and Jean—died as young women.

During one of those sad times in their lives—it could have been after the death of one of their children—Twain said to Livy, "If it comforts you to lean on the Christian faith, do so."

"But I can't, Youth; I haven't any," she sadly replied.

Twain felt responsible for causing Livy to lose her faith and the thought came back to haunt him many times after her death in 1904.

Mark Twain loved Livy devotedly, but apparently his unbelieving attitude had an effect on her that even he didn't want.[1]

One of our best-known American preachers and theologians was Horace Bushnell (1802-1876). In his early years, Bushnell believed that a child ought to grow up as a "Christian" and he opposed the idea of a personal, spiritual crisis in children. Bushnell also helped select the Berkley site for the University of California campus.

But while a law student at Yale, Bushnell was an unbeliever. During a great spiritual revival that was sweeping the Yale campus, Bushnell became disturbed when he learned that many of the undergraduate students refused to attend the services because he didn't attend them.

One day he faced his unbelief squarely. "If I do not believe in Christ, what do I believe in?" he asked himself. He then firmly decided that there had to be an absolute difference between right and wrong. Then he asked himself, "If I put myself on the side of what is right, do I tend to follow it regardless of the consequences?"

His answer was that he had not, but he would. It was then and there he dedicated himself to the principle of doing what is right.

After Bushnell had been in the ministry forty-seven years, having moved a great distance from the unbelief of his immature years, he confessed, "Better than I know any man in Hartford, I know Jesus Christ."[2]

1. Clarence Macartney, *Macartney's Illustrations*, (New York and Nashville: Abingdon-Cokesbury Press, 1945), 225.
2. Charles L. Allen, *Roads To Radiant Living*, (Old Tappan, N. J.: Fleming H. Revell, Co., 1961), 130.

Witness/Witnessing

And ye shall be witnesses unto me (Acts 1:8).

In 1855, A Sunday School teacher named Ezra Kimball witnessed to a nineteen-year-old shoe clerk named Dwight L. Moody. Young Moody prayed and asked Jesus to come into his life but when he tried to join the church, they turned him down because he was too ignorant about biblical things. A year later he was admitted to church membership and became a Sunday School teacher. Later, he committed himself to God's call to the ministry.

Moody was preaching in England on one occasion in the church where the cultured preacher and theologian Frederick B. Meyer was pastor. Meyer was uncomfortable with Moody's poor grammar and deathbed stories and squirmed through Moody's sermon. Meyer was particularly uncomfortable when Moody told about a Sunday School teacher who was dying of cancer but led every member of his Sunday School class to Jesus before his death. Talking to one of his church ladies later, Pastor Meyer asked her how things were going with her Sunday School class and she replied everything was tremendous since she had heard Moody preach. "I have led every member of my Sunday School class to Jesus," she joyously responded.

Moody fired F. B. Meyer's spirit and later, when Meyer was on an evangelistic tour across the United States, young Wilbur Chapman heard him. Chapman was a discouraged young minister, but the Holy Spirit spoke through F. B. Meyer and encouraged Chapman.

Chapman became an outstanding evangelist and Bible teacher. As his work expanded, Chapman needed an assistant so he chose a poorly educated young man named Billy Sunday who was working for the YMCA. Sunday became an evangelist and, it is said, led more than a million people to the Savior.

In 1924, Billy Sunday preached in Charlotte, North Carolina, and a revival meeting broke out. As a result of the revival, a prayer group formed and began praying that God would send a great revival to their city.

In answer to their prayers, Mordecai Ham came to Charlotte and preached and a great revival broke out. One night in 1934, two young men attended the services and were saved. One was Grady Wilson and the other was sixteen-year-old Billy Graham.

"There is a great sinner in this place tonight," Ham said in opening his message that night. Billy Graham said he thought to himself, *Mother's been telling him about me.* Both Billy Graham and Grady Wilson were saved during Ham's revival meeting in Charlotte and together they formed the well-known Billy Graham Evangelistic Team. And Billy Graham has preached to more people than any person in history.[1]

Dr. Alexander Duff was the first missionary sent to India by the Church of Scotland. He sailed for India in 1830 and was shipwrecked twice before he arrived. He left India in 1863 and spent the remainder of his life lecturing across his native Scotland in colleges and universities on behalf of world missions.

During one such lecture in a university, Duff fainted and was carried from the pulpit by loving arms. When he revived he asked, "Where am I? What am I doing?"

When told that he had been lecturing on India, Dr. Duff replied: "I must go back and continue."

But his friends insisted, "If you go back, you will die."

But Dr. Duff replied, "I will die if I don't go back."

Helped to a chair where he remained seated as he continued his plea for mission volunteers, Dr. Duff said to the students: "Will any of you young men or women give your lives to carry the gospel of Christ to India? If you won't, then I will go back that they may know that in England there is one man who cares for their souls."[2]

Knowing the power of the twenty-six-letter alphabet, Benjamin Franklin said: "Give me twenty-six lead soldiers and I will conquer the world."

Few things are more powerful than the printed page. In the fifteenth century, Richard Gibbs wrote a tract titled "The Bruised Reed" which led to the conversion of Richard Baxter. Baxter became one of England's greatest preachers.

Baxter wrote more than 100 books. One of them, *The Call To The Unconverted*, led tens of thousands to Christ, including Philip Doddridge. Doddridge was called to preach and one of his books, *The Rise and Progress of Religion*, led William Wilberforce to Christ. Wilberforce probably did more to abolish slavery from the British colonies than any man in England's history. His book, *A Practical View of Christianity*, led Leigh Richmond to Jesus. Richmond's booklet, *The Dairyman's Daughter*, brought thousands to Jesus.[3]

1. Zig Ziglar, *Confessions Of A Happy Christian* (New York: Bantam Books, 1978), 148-149.

2. J. B. Fowler, Sermons, "Come Before Winter," 8.

3. William S. Deal, *Paths of Revival* (no publisher given, 1984), 1.

Index

ADOPTION. 13
  Barnhouse, Donald Grey. 13
  Douglas, Lloyd. 13
  "The Robe" 13
  Wuest, Kenneth 13
ANGELS 15
  Graham, Billy. 15
  Mitchell, Dr. S. W. 15
  Paton, John G. 16
  Rooney, Mickey. 15
ANGER 17
  Carver, George Washington 18
  Gulledge, Jack 18
  Lincoln, Abraham 17
  Seward, William Henry. 17
  Tuskegee Institute 17
  Washington, Booker T. 17
  Williams, Dr. Redford B. 18
ANXIOUS (SEE CAREFUL) 39
ASSURANCE/SECURITY 19
  Clough, Arthur Hugh 19
  Garfield, James A. 20
  Golden Gate Bridge. 19
  King, Guy. 19
  Lincoln, Abraham 20
  Criswell, W. A. 20
BAPTIZE/BAPTISM. 23
  Carey, William. 24
  Gulledge, Jack 24
  River Jordan. 24
  Judson, Ann & Adoniram. 24
  Metropolitan Baptist Tabernacle . . . 23
  Spurgeon, Charles Haddon 23
BELIEVE. 26
  Blondin. 26
  Bryson, Harold T. 26
  Hightower, James E. 26
  Jones, Edgar Dewitt. 27
  Niagara Falls 26
  Paton, John G. 27
  Weatherhead, Leslie. 26
BIBLE (SEE SCRIPTURE). 161
BLOOD 29
  Barclay, William 30
  Caesar. 29
  Davis, W. D. 30
  Escalus 29
  Havergal, Frances Ridley 29
  Huegal, F. J. 29

  Luther, Martin. 29
  Ockenga, Harold John. 30
  Satan. 29
BORN AGAIN 32
  Angell, Roy 34
  Finney, Charles G. 33
  Gehrig, Henry Louis "Lou" 33
  Jacquess, Rev. James F. 32
  Lincoln, Abraham 32
  Lincoln, Mrs. Abraham. 32
  Lincoln, Eddie 32
  Owen, G. Frederick. 32
  Pickering, Hy. 32
  Tarkington, Louis Fletcher 34
BURDENS. 36
  Beethoven 37
  Booth, William. 37
  Byron, Lord 37
  Carver, George Washington 37
  Edison, Thomas A. 37
  Fitzgerald, Edward 36
  Hawthorne, Nathaniel. 36
  Keller, Helen 37
  Lincoln, Abraham 37
  Milton, John. 37
  Pasteur, Louis. 37
  Scott, Sir Walter. 37
  Leland Stanford Junior University . . 36
  Washington, Booker T. 37
CAREFUL/ANXIOUS 39
  Bowen, Catherine. 39
  Carlyle, Thomas. 40
  Churchill, Winston. 39
  Emerson, Ralph Waldo. 40
  Holmes, Oliver Wendell 39
  Lincoln, Abraham 39
  Luther, Martin. 39
  Prochnow, Herbert V. 39
  Van Gogh, Vincent 39
CHRIST (SEE JESUS) 95
CHURCH. 44
  Angell, Roy 41
  Booth, William. 42
  Conwell, Russell H. 43
  Ely, Virginia. 42
  Grace Baptist Church 43
  Grey, J. D. 42
  Kipling, Rudyard. 42
  Paderewski 42

190   Illustrating Great Words of the New Testament

Rubinstein, Arthur. 42
Temple University 43
Thorn, W. E. 41
Wyatt, Hattie. 43
CROSS 45
Bell, Irene. 45
Campbell, R. C. 45
Garcia, Jesus 47
Hefley, James. 47
Lee, R. G. 46
Morriss, John B. 45
Munkacsky, Michael 47
O'Brien, Randall 45
Villers, Thomas, J. 48
DEATH 49
Hickok, James Butler "Wild Bill" . . 50
Calamity Jane. 50
Luther, Martin. 49
McCall, Jack. 50
Michaelangelo. 49
King Philip of Macedon 51
Polycarp 49
Wesley, John 49
DEVIL (SEE SATAN). 158
EASTER (SEE RESURRECTION) . 146
EXAMPLE. 52
Brainerd, David 52
Carey, Williams 52
Ely, Virginia. 53
Glover, Robert H. 52
Judson, Adoniram 52
Martyn, Henry. 52
Spurgeon, Charles Haddon 53
FAITH 55
Baker, Robert A. 56
Carroll, Dr. B. H. 56
Muller, George. 55
Southwestern   Baptist   Theological
Seminary. 56
FEAR 58
Fosdick, Harry Emerson. 58
Hamilton, J. Wallace. 59
McPherson, Nenien C., Jr. 59
Murrow, Edward R. 58
Peale, Dr. Norman Vincent 59
Sadler, Dr. William 59
Wellborn, Charles 58
FORGIVENESS 60
Angell, Roy 60
Cronin, A. J. 60, 61

University of Glasgow, Scotland . . . 60
Grenfell, Sir Wilfred 61
Middleton, R. L. 61
FOUNDATION 63
Peale, Norman Vincent 63
GOD. 64
Augustine 65
Dehoney, Wayne 64
St. Francis of Assisi. 65
Keller, Helen 64
Lee, R. G. 64
Morrison, Cressya 65
Sullivan, Anne 64
GRACE 67
Astor, John Jacob 68
Burke, Valentine 69
Jones, Sam 68
Longfellow, Henry Wadsworth. 68
Michaelangelo. 68
Moody, Dwight L. 67, 69
Pierce, Earle V. 67
Sistine Chapel. 68
Wright Brothers. 68
Wuest, Kenneth 67
HEAVEN. 70
Angell, Roy 71
Battle of Bull Run 73
Bee, Gen., Barnard 73
Bronner, Ben 71
Cash, Jack. 70
Cash, Johnny 70
Hooker, Gen. Joseph. 73
Jackson, Stonewall. 73
Lee, Robert E. 73
Metts, Andy & Mary. 72
Moody, Dwight L. 71
Moody, Will. 71
Orrick, Beluah Carroll. 72
HELL 75
Buren, Martin Van 76
Jackson, Andrew 76
Kendall, Amos. 76
Studd, C. T. 76
HOME 78
Angell, Roy 79, 80
Beecher, Lyman. 79
Brooks, Phillips 79
Carlyle, Thomas. 78
Fitzgerald, F. Scott 80
Franklin, Benjamin 79

"The Great Gatsby" 80
Gulledge, Jack 79
LaBeff, Margie................. 79
Peale, Norman Vincent.......... 73
Salty the dog 79
Shakespeare, William........... 79
Stowe, Harriet Beecher 79
Tennyson, Alfred............... 79
"The Last Tycoon" 80
Queen Victoria................. 78
Washington, George 79
Wesley, John 79
Westminster Abbey 78
HONESTY..................... 81
Grant, Ulysses S............... 81
Lee, Robert E................. 81
Macartney, Clarence 82
Washington, George 82
Weems, Rev. Mason 82
HOPE........................ 84
Browne, Benjamin.............. 85
Fields, L..................... 84
Hill, Napoleon 84
McCartney, Clarence............ 84
Mendelssohn, Felix 85
Tate Gallery in London.......... 84
HUMBLE/HUMILITY 87
Baker, E. D................... 88
Beethoven.................... 87
Big Ben...................... 88
Douglas, Stephen A............. 88
Lincoln, Abraham 88
MacPherson, Ian 88
Mitropoulos, Dimitri............ 87
Middleton, R. L................ 87
Parker, Joseph 88
Spurgeon, Charles Haddon 88
Wood, Ralph L................ 87
HUMILITY (SEE HUMBLE)....... 87
IDLE/IDLENESS................ 90
Welch, W. K.................. 90
IMMORTALITY 91
Bonnell, John Sutherland 91
Chalmers, Thomas.............. 91
Hugo, Victor.................. 91
Ingersoll, Robert 92
Kant, Emmanuel 91
Lincoln, Abraham 91
Lincoln, Willie................. 91
Dr. Vinton 91

JEALOUS/JEALOUSY 93
Dryden, John 94
Lee, R. G.................... 93
MacPherson, Ian 93
Shakespeare, William............ 94
JESUS/CHRIST 95
Alexander the Great 95, 96
Aristotle 95
Augustas, Caesar 96
Bonaparte, Napoleon............ 95
Browne, Benjamin P............. 95
Buddha...................... 96
Caesar, Julius.................. 95
Cicero 95
da Vinci, Leonardo 95
Encyclopedia Britannica 95
Graham, Billy.................. 97
Grant, J. Ralph 96, 97
Hefley, James.................. 95
Krishna...................... 96
"The Last Supper" painting 95
"One Solitary Life" 96
Perseus 96
Plato 96
Pythagoras 96
Wells, H. G................... 95
Zoroaster..................... 96
JOY......................... 99
Barclay, William 100
Browne, Benjamin 100
Cuyler, Theodore.............. 101
Grant, Dr. J. Ralph............. 99
Jenkins, Dr. Millard A.......... 100
Nelson, John.................. 100
Rees, Dr. Paul 99
Rodeheaver, Homer............. 100
Spurgeon, Charles H............ 101
Wesley, John 100
JUDGMENT................... 102
"Acres of Diamonds" 102
Angell, Roy 102
Barton, Bruce................. 102
Booth, William................ 103
Conwell, Russell............... 102
Grant, J. Ralph 104
Philip of Macedon 103
KIND/KINDNESS 105
Astor, William Waldorf......... 107
Boldt, George C. 107
Davis, Jefferson 107

Durer, Albert 105
Lee, Robert E. 107
Middleton, R. L. 105
"Praying Hands" 105
Waldorf-Astoria Hotel. 107
Washington, George 107
Whiting, General 107
LAUGH/LAUGHTER 109
Carlyle, Thomas. 110
Goethe, Johann 110
Grey, Dr. J. D.. 109
Lamb, Charles 109
Thackery, William. 109
Thorn, W. E. 109
LOST 111
"The Adventures of Huckleberry
Finn". 112
"The Adventures of Tom Sawyer". 112
Brown, Benjamin. 112
Bryan, William Jennings 111
Burr, Aaron 112
Clemens, Samuel Langhorne. 112
Darrow, Clarence. 111
Edwards, Jonathan. 112
Hamilton, Alexander 113
Henley, William Ernest. 113
Jefferson, Thomas 112
Princeton College (University) 112
Smith, Rodney "Gipsy" 111
Twain, Mark. 112
Whitherspoon, Dr. John 112
LOVE 114
Barrett, Elizabeth. 115
Browning, Robert. 115
Grenfell, Sir Wilfred 114
Johnson, Ellen C.. 116
Lamb, Charles and Mary 116
Middleton, R. L. 116
Mataafa. 117
Osbourne, Fanny 114
"Raisin In The Sun" 114
Stevenson, Robert Louis 114, 117
"Treasure Island" 117
Truett, Dr. George W. 116
MAN/WOMAN 119
Barclay, William 121
Bentley, John 120
Carver, George Washington 120
Graham, Billy. 120
Grant, Ulysses S. 121

Hobbs, Herschel H. 119
Lightfoot, Professor 119
Muretus. 121
Porter, Henry Alford. 121
St. Paul's Cathedral 120
Ussher, (Archbishop) James 119
Waters, Ethel 120
MERCY 123
Battle of Bull Run 124
Baxter, Richard 123, 124
Copernicus, Nicolaus. 123
Dean, Robert J. 124
Foster, Elon 124
Mullins, E. Y.. 123
MIRACLES 126
Bartley, James 126
NEGLECT 129
Allen, Charles L. 130
PEACE. 131
Barker, Eric 131
Battle of New Orleans. 132
Jackson, Andrew 131
Boshoff, Norm 131
Lord, Dr. F. Townley 132
Peale, Norman Vincent 132
PRAYER 134
Brainerd, David 135
Browne, Benjamin P.. 135
Finn, Huckleberry 134
Finney, Charles 135
Grant, Ulysses S. 134
Howard, Gen., O. O. 134
Hunter, Dr. Wyatt. 135
Jackson, Stonewall. 134
Judson, Adoniram 135
Luther, Martin. 135
Moody, Dwight L.. 135
Muller, George. 135
Twain, Mark. 134
Whitefield, George. 135
PRIDE 137
Burr, Aaron 137
Hamilton, Alexander 137
Jefferson, Thomas 137
Luccock, Halford. 138
Napoleon. 138
Pope Pius VII. 138
REAPING (SEE SOWING) 171
REDEEM/REDEMPTION 139
Barnhouse, Donald Grey. 139

Lincoln, Abraham 140
Lloyd, Edward 141
Lloyd's of London 141
Seward, William Henry 140
Thayer, Joseph H. 139
Wallace, Irving 141
Wallechinsky, David 141
Wuest, Kenneth S. 139
REPENT/REPENTANCE 143
Angell, Roy 143
Ayers, Dr. T. W. 144
Defoe, Daniel 143
Lee, R. G. 145
Macartney, Clarence E. 143
Marney, Carlyle 145
Mead, J. Earl 144
"Robinson Crusoe" 143
Strong, Augustus H. 143
RESURRECTION/EASTER 146
Brisbane, Arthur 149
De Gama, Vasco 148
Queen Elizabeth I 147
Faraday, Michael 148
Grant, J. Ralph 146, 148
Knight, Walter B. 149
Morgan, G. Campbell 146
Raleigh, Sir Walter 147
SACRIFICE 150
Edwards, Jonathan Hall 150
Judson, Adoniram 150
Judson, Ann 151
Newell, Harriet Atwood 150
Newell, Samuel 150
Tizard, Leslie J. 150
SALVATION 153
Cowper, William 153
Dixon, Dr. A. C. 156
Erikson, Erik H. 154
Lee, Dr. R. G. 156
Luther, Martin 154
Middleton, R. L. 156
Newton, John 153
Staupitz, Johann 154
Unwin, Morley 153
Wesley, John 155
Wesley, Samuel 155
SATAN/DEVIL 158
Carlyle, Thomas 158
Defoe, Daniel 159
Emerson, Ralph Waldo 158
Hobbs, Herschel H. 158
Knight, Walter B. 160
Luther, Martin 158
"Robinson Crusoe" 159
SECURITY (SEE ASSURANCE) 19
SCRIPTURE/BIBLE 161
"A Christmas Carol" 165
"A Tale of Two Cities" 165
Dickens, Charles 165
Duff, Alexander 163
Franklin, Benjamin 163
Gladstone, William 163
Grant, Ulysses S. 163
Hastings, Robert J. 162, 163
Henry, Patrick 163
Hultgren, Warren 164
Jackson, Andrew 163
Keller, Helen 163
Lee, Robert E. 163
Lincoln, Abraham 162
Luther, Martin 163
Napoleon 163
Scott, Sir Walter 163
Sizoo, Joseph 162
Washington, George 163
Wesley, John 164
Wilson, Woodrow 163
SIN 166
Bandinelli, Pietro 167
Beecher, Henry Ward 168
Blackwelder, Dr. Oscar 167
Cranford, Clarence 167
Cromwell, Oliver 167
da Vinci, Leonardo 167
Hightower, James 168
Hugo, Victor 168
"The Last Supper" 167
Lee, R. G. 169
MacPherson, Ian 166
Maclaren, Alexander 166
Moody, Dwight L. 166
Supreme Court Building 167
Tilton, Elizabeth 168
"The Toilers of the Sea" 168
Tracy, Dr. Nat 166
Tuck, William P. 168
SOWING/REAPING 171
Angell, Roy 171
Augustine 172
Lewis, Sinclair 173

Middleton, R. L. 171
Stidger, Dr. William 173
SUFFERING/TRIALS 175
   Angell, Roy 177
   Beethoven 175
   Bunyan, John 175
   Disraeli, Benjamin 176
   Edison, Thomas 176
   "Ivanhoe" 176
   Keats, John................... 175
   Keller, Helen 176
   Lincoln, Abraham 175
   Lyte, Henry Francis............ 176
   Macartney, Clarence 175
   "Pilgrim's Progress" 175
   Scott, Sir Walter.............. 176
   Strombeck, George............. 177
TEMPTATION 178
   Burns, Robert................. 178
   "The Call of the Wild" 179
   Hart, Emma 179
   London, Jack 179
   Macartney, Clarence 178, 179
   Nelson, Horatio 179
   Orpheus...................... 178
   Romney, George 179
   Tennyson, Lord 179
   Ulysses 178
TRIALS (SEE SUFFERING) 175
TRUST........................ 181
   Finegan, Jack 182

Havergal, Frances Ridley 181
Kraft, James L. 182
Macartney, Clarence 181
Moody, Dwight L............... 181
Taylor, Hudson 181
UNBELIEF 184
   "The   Adventures   of   Huckleberry
Finn"........................... 184
   "The Adventures of Tom Sawyer". 184
   Bushnell, Horace 184
   Clemens, Samuel Langhorne...... 184
   Macartney, Clarence 184
   Twain, Mark.................. 184
WITNESS...................... 186
   Baxter, Richard 188
   Chapman, William.............. 186
   Doddridge, Philip.............. 188
   Duff, Dr. Alexander 187
   Franklin, Benjamin 188
   Gibbs, Richard................. 188
   Graham, Billy.................. 187
   Ham, Mordecai 187
   Kimball, Ezra.................. 186
   Meyer, Frederick B............. 186
   Moody, Dwight L............... 186
   Richmond, Leigh............... 188
   Sunday, Billy 187
   Wilberforce, William 188
   Wilson, Grady 187
WOMAN (SEE MAN/WOMAN)... 119